W9-AFC-622

Contents

PAGE	UNIT TITLE	TOPICS	USEFUL LANGUAGE AND STRUCTURES
5	**1 Introduction to air communications**	**Setting the scene** **Basics of radio communication** **Introduction to non-routine situations**	ICAO alphabet and numbers Asking for repetition Questions and short answers Talking about imaginary situations
13	**2 Pre-flight**	**Pre-flight checks** **Delays and problems** **Local conditions**	Asking for more time Giving a reason Saying what you're going to do Saying there's a problem Requesting action
21	**3 Ground movements**	**Airport markings and airside vehicles** **Taxiing and holding** **Weather problems**	Permission, obligation, prohibition Explaining problems Saying a problem has been solved
29	**4 Departure, climbing, and cruising**	**Take-off** **Encountering traffic** **Warnings about hazards**	Checking and asking for an alternative Using prepositions of position Saying how much Warnings and requests Time expressions Giving reasons
37	**5 En route events**	**Operational situations** **Unusual events** **Medical situations**	Comparing things Talking about probability
45	**6 Contact and approach**	**Descent** **Weather conditions** **Approach and landing problems**	Talking about time Explaining changes in plans Talking about cause and effect Requests
53	**7 Landing**	**Landing incidents** **Circuit joining** **Landing hazards**	Reported speech Making suggestions Offering help Giving advice or opinions
61	**8 On the ground**	**Taxiing** **Getting to the gate** **Clear communication**	Explaining what happened Saying what will happen

PAGE	APPENDIX
68	**Test yourself!**
70	**Partner Files**
74	**Answer key**
84	**Transcripts**

About the book

English for Aviation has been developed specifically for people who work in the aviation industry and need to comply with the International Civil Aviation Organization's (ICAO's) language proficiency requirements. It supports standard phraseology and builds upon it to help improve plain English in the skill areas specified by ICAO: pronunciation, structure, vocabulary, fluency, comprehension, and interactions.

English for Aviation covers a range of subjects associated with flying and the aviation industry. The book is organized in the sequence of a flight, starting with an introductory unit, followed by pre-flight, ground movements, departure, cruising, en route events, contact and approach, landing, and end-of-flight ground movements. Pilots and air traffic controllers will find the book useful for improving their plain English, but anyone working in aviation – ground staff, emergency services, or administrators, for example – who wants to improve their English ability will benefit from **English for Aviation**. Units from the book work independently and can be selected according to the needs and interests of the course participants. **English for Aviation** is also ideal for self-study.

Each unit begins with a **Starter**, which consists of a short exercise or a quiz and serves as an introduction to the topic of the unit. Practical exercises, listening extracts, industry-specific texts as well as numerous photos and illustrations help you to acquire key vocabulary and expressions. Realistic role-plays give you the opportunity to put all you have learned into practice. Each unit closes with an **Output** activity, an article related to the topic of the unit followed by questions for reflection and discussion. The book finishes up with a fun quiz to **Test yourself!** on some of the facts and figures discussed over the previous eight units.

English for Aviation is accompanied by two disks. The **Audio CD** contains all the listening for the book. The **Audio CD** can be played through the audio player on your computer or through a conventional CD player. The **CD ROM** contains interactive exercises to practise **structure**, **vocabulary**, and **listening comprehension**. There is also an A–Z word list with all the key words that appear in the book. Visit www.oup.com/elt/express for ICAO compliancy practice tests.

In the appendix of **English for Aviation** you will find the **Partner Files** for the role-plays and the **Answer key** so that you can check your own answers if you are working alone. There are also **Transcripts** of the listening extracts.

1 Introduction to air communications

STARTER

Use arrows (⟷) to link the people who talk to each other.

PILOT G-SC27

PILOT FLIGHT 71

CABIN CREW FLIGHT 71

TOWER CONTROLLER

CO-PILOT FLIGHT 71

PASSENGERS FLIGHT 71

AUDIO

2

COMPREHENSION

1 **Air communications are vital for the safety of air travel. Listen to the two exchanges and answer the questions.**

1 a Which stand is 363 on?
   b Where does the controller think 363 is?
   c Which numbers and letters are incorrectly pronounced?
2 a Which flight level is X7420 climbing to?
   b What is the altitude of X7420?
   c What two words does the controller confuse?

Look at the six language areas on page 2. Listen again to the two exchanges and look at the transcripts on page 84. Find an example of a difficulty with each language area.

Discuss these questions with a partner.

1   Have you had any similar experiences?
2   What communication problems have you had when talking to foreign pilots or controllers?

AUDIO

3

PRONUNCIATION

2   Listen and repeat.

ICAO ALPHABET AND NUMBERS					
A	Alpha	K	Kilo	U	Uniform
B	Bravo	L	Lima	V	Victor
C	Charlie	M	Mike	W	Whiskey
D	Delta	N	November	X	X-ray
E	Echo	O	Oscar	Y	Yankee
F	Foxtrot	P	Papa	Z	Zulu
G	Golf	Q	Quebec		
H	Hotel	R	Romeo		
I	India	S	Sierra		
J	Juliett	T	Tango		
0	zero	4	fower	8	ait
1	wun	5	fife	9	niner
2	too	6	six		
3	tree	7	seven		

oo (hundred) hundred
ooo (thousand) tousand
. (decimal) dayseemal

British CAA	ICAO/Global
FL 100 = flight level one hundred	FL 100 = flight level one zero zero

AUDIO

4

3   Listen to the sample message and repeat.

> *London Control, Express 164. Flight Level 100. Heading 345. ETA Belfast 0839.*

INTERACTIONS

Work with a partner to pass and record messages. If you are not sure about the message, ask for clarification. Repeat *Say again* until you have understood.

ASKING FOR REPETITION	
Repeat entire message	**Repeat specific item**
Say again.	Say again flight level.
	Say again all before heading.
	Say again all after flight level.
	Say again flight level to ETA.

PARTNER FILES ➤ Partner A   File 1, p. 70
Partner B   File 8, p. 72

AUDIO

5

Listen and check. Then compare what you wrote with the information your partner read.

QUESTIONS AND SHORT ANSWERS

Are you on stand C63 or C61?	I'm/We're on stand C61.
Is the radio on the correct frequency?	Yes, it is./No, it isn't.
Have you set the QNH?	Yes./Yes, I have./No, I haven't.
Has the weather improved?	Yes, it has./No, it hasn't.
Do you have the flight plan?	Yes, I've got it here./No, I don't.
Do you know where John is?	Yes, I do./No, I don't.
Did the bird strike cause any damage?	Yes, it did./No, it didn't.

4 **Put the words in the right order to make questions. Then answer them.**

1 you a a controller pilot Are or ?
2 speak other languages you Do any ?
3 abroad ever you been Have ?
4 plane travel last When by you did ?
5 your provide training company courses English Does ?
6 English in minutes the ten your last improved Has ?

American English	**British English**
airplane	aeroplane

5 **Match the two parts of the sentences to make six reasons why international communications may be difficult.**

1	ATCOs and pilots may speak	a	English words are used.
2	There may be very poor reception	b	in their own language.
3	Extra and unnecessary	c	or no standard phraseology.
4	ATCOs or pilots may sometimes	d	on the radio.
5	Non-routine situations have little	e	use plain English.
6	ATCOs or pilots may not understand	f	standard English phraseology.

AUDIO 6

6 **Listen to five exchanges. Write the number of the exchange next to the description below. Then tick how often you expect to hear each of these in your work. Then discuss your answers with a partner.**

	always	often	usually	some-times	occasionally	rarely	never
a ____ standard phraseology	❑	❑	❑	❑	❑	❑	❑
b ____ non-standard phraseology	❑	❑	❑	❑	❑	❑	❑
c _1_ unnecessary English words	❑	❑	❑	❑	❑	❑	❑
d ____ plain English	❑	❑	❑	❑	❑	❑	❑
e ____ local language	❑	❑	❑	❑	❑	❑	❑

AUDIO 7

7 **Listen to the exchange as a long haul flight approaches its destination. Answer the questions.**

1 What is the main communication problem?
2 How did the pilot try to help the controller understand?
3 How did the controller deal with the situation?

VOCABULARY

8 **Listen again. From each pair of words, tick the word you hear.**

1	violent	vibration	5	aggressive	angry
2	rude	unruly	6	ground	around
3	hit	hate	7	services	service
4	drink	drunk	8	remain	remove

9 **What is the problem on board the aircraft? Use words you have selected in exercise 8 to make sentences.**

1 The passenger was _____ , _____, and _____ .
2 The passenger _____ a crew member.
3 The pilot wanted to get on the _____ as soon as possible.

Have you ever had a difficult communication? What did you do?

Yes, I have. I had a medical emergency. The pilot asked for ...
The controller asked me to ...
No, I haven't.

10 **Use words from exercise 6 to complete the article.**

SAFETY SENSE

Dealing with non-routine events

<u>Occasionally</u> [1] a pilot may be able to use _____ [2] phraseology for a non-routine event, but he will _____ [3] have to use _____ [4] English. In this event he had to use _____ [5] phraseology but tried to assist the controller by not using any _____ [6] English words and by using several different words with a similar meaning.

The radio transmission was good, but the controller could not understand the problem as he _____ [7] dealt with domestic flights and _____ [8] spoke to a foreign pilot. This can _____ [9] be a problem for controllers as they get little practice with spoken English and _____ [10] speak to local pilots in the _____ [11] language. A non-English speaker will _____ [12] be alone in this situation and help will _____ [13] be available.

Answer the questions.

1 How often do you use English for your job?
2 How often do you speak English to:
   a non-native speakers?
   b native English speakers?
3 How often do you listen to the radio or watch TV in English?
4 What is your best English skill: listening, speaking, reading, or writing? Which would you most like to improve?
5 Have you ever had difficulty trying to speak English? What was the outcome?

VOCABULARY

PHRASAL VERBS

Phrasal verbs have two parts. The meaning may be clear from the two parts:
*Please **come in** and **sit down**.*

The meaning may not be clear from the two parts:
*Did the tanker **break down**?*

11 **Complete the two exchanges with the words from the box.**

check out • keep up • stays up • get back • come in • get to • pass over

Exchange 1

Approach   Wolfair 60, good morning. Identified. Proceeding into Alba. Vectoring 05.

Wolfair 60   Direct Alba 05. Wolfair 60. Can I _____ [1] this high speed a bit longer? Wolfair 60.

Approach   Wolfair 60, for the time being, yes. I'll _____ [2] to you in a minute.

Exchange 2

Tower   B67, will you let me know what your intentions are for the main landing gear?

B67   Roger. We'll try to lower the gear again, but if I'm still unable to release the nose gear – if it still _____ [3] – then we'll land with all three up. B67.

Tower   B67, do you want to _____ [4] for a low pass? We can _____ [5] your landing gear when you _____ [6].

B67   OK, roger. B67.

Tower   B67, have you got the field in sight?

B67   B67, affirm. When I _____ [7] you the gear should be down. B67.

Tower   B67, roger. OK, make a low pass over runway 23 for a landing gear check.

AUDIO
8

Listen and check.

12 **Find words or phrases in the exchanges with the same meaning as these words.**

1   attempt
2   Can you see the airport?
3   fly low over the runway
4   a little more time
5   now and for a few minutes

6   tell me
7   inspect
8   Request permission ...
9   Would you like to ... ?
10   You are on my radar screen.

FLUENCY

13 **Underline the plain English phrases in exercise 11. Then answer the questions for each exchange.**

Exchange 1

1   Are the plain English phrases necessary?
2   What does the controller agree to?
3   Can you replace the plain English with correct phraseology?

Exchange 2

1   Which gear is a problem?
2   What does the controller suggest?
3   What will the pilot do if the problem remains?

14 **What would you do in these situations? Compare your ideas with a partner.**

Situation 1

At a foreign airport you are the pilot of a passenger jet waiting to take off from runway 09. You are number two to depart. An inbound A320 lands on runway 09 and aircraft number one ahead of you departs. All communications between the pilots and ATC are in the local language. You believe you heard wind shear and high wind speeds mentioned. You are now cleared, in English, to line up and take off. ATC do not mention wind shear.

Situation 2

You are an approach controller in a busy airport. An incoming English-speaking pilot has requested a priority landing for a heavy aircraft. He has repeated the request but you still cannot understand the reason.

Situation 3

You are the pilot of a passenger aircraft approaching runway 18. You were cleared for ILS approach and had instructions to continue. You made calls at the outer marker and 2 nautical miles but received no reply. You are now at 500 feet and see a light aircraft in the one o'clock position at the same level, passing right to left. You have heard communications in the local language.

Situation 4

You are an approach controller and have twice issued instructions to an approaching B757 but have had no response. The plane is at the outer marker and appears to be on course for landing as instructed.

TALKING ABOUT IMAGINARY SITUATIONS
I would ask about wind shear. I would give permission to land.

In each case what would you say to deal with the situation?

15 **Think of a situation in your experience where there was confusion or a misunderstanding.**

1   Who was involved?
2   What was the problem?
3   How was it resolved?

Read the report and answer the questions.

DESCENT CONFUSION

An airliner had to divert to an alternate airport because of engine problems. The pilot did not declare an emergency but requested a descent to 2000 feet in order to re-start the engine. The plane had also lost pressurisation but the pilot was unable to explain this to ATC. Controllers were concerned that the pilot wanted to descend so low but were unable to make the pilot understand their questions. They then asked 'Can you just advise me – are you descending to use fuel?'

The flight crew misinterpreted this as 'Do you have enough fuel?' and replied 'Yes, yes. We are descending with fuel enough and everything is OK'. Because the pilot had not understood the question, the reply confused the controller even more.

Fortunately, the controller guessed there was an emergency and the aircraft was put on a 7700 squawk. He transferred the aircraft to its own frequency. The aircraft landed safely but the poor understanding and communication from the pilot was reported to the authorities.

OVER TO YOU

Do you know any stories of a plane making a rapid descent following depressurization? What happened?
Have you experienced a pilot needing to use fuel before landing? What was the situation?

2 Pre-flight

STARTER

It is important for controllers and pilots to be able to identify an aircraft type so they know what it is capable of. How many of these aircraft can you identify?

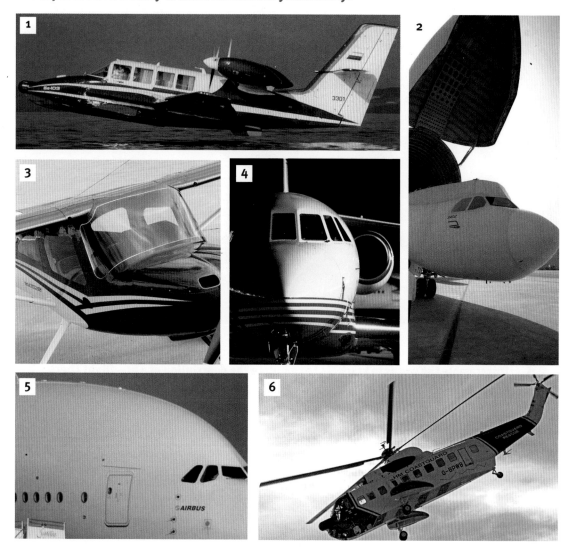

VOCABULARY

1 Match the words to make plane parts. Can you find all of the parts in the pictures above?

A		
1 tail	a	door
2 cargo	b	assembly
3 engine	c	cowling

B		
1 trailing	a	light
2 access	b	hatch
3 navigation	c	edge

C		
1 under	a	edge
2 landing	b	light
3 leading	c	carriage

2 Label the parts of the plane 1–18 with the words a–r.

a   nose
b   windscreen
c   aerial
d   aileron
e   spoiler
f   flap
g   slat
h   winglet
i   fuselage

j   rudder
k   elevator
l   tail fin
m   tyre
n   engine
o   emergency exit
p   radome
q   light
r   outboard slats

British English	American English
aerial	antenna
tyre	tire
windscreen	windshield
fin	vertical stabilizer
tailplane	horizontal stabilizer

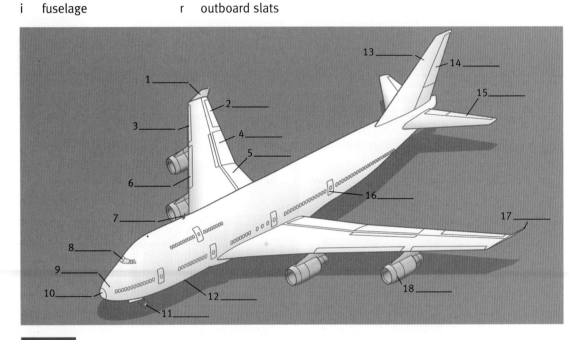

FLUENCY

3 Unscramble the words in brackets to complete the description of a pre-flight check.

Pre-flight

Before flying, the pilot carefully (khcecs)_____¹ the aircraft. He looks at the external (causrfes)_____² for signs of damage. A plane may be damaged by a bird (ritske)_____³ or (gnilghtin)_____⁴ strike or contact with any other (gorfein)_____⁵ object, or by service (sveichle)_____⁶ on the ground. Bent or distorted panels may be a visual indication of hidden (madgae) _____⁷ to the airframe.

He then checks the nose (crundagerirae) _____⁸ for excessive (arew) _____⁹ or cuts on the tyres.

He inspects the (deliagn)_____¹⁰ edge of the wing for damage and checks the fastenings on the (eeginn)_____¹¹ cowling. He examines the visible fan (sladeb)_____¹² on the engines.

Moving along the (slegeafu)_____¹³ to the tail he does the same visual checks over all surfaces before ensuring that all cargo (rodos)_____¹⁴ and access (stacheh)_____¹⁵ are securely fastened.

4 Pre-flight checks continue on the flight deck. Name as many items as you can in these pictures.

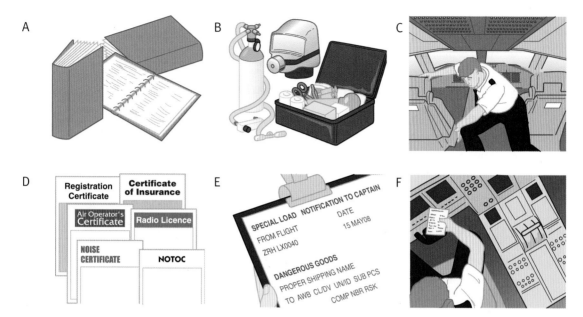

5 Match the sentence halves. Then match each sentence to a picture above.

1 Certificates and other documents must
2 Documentation for any unusual cargo or
3 Instruction manuals may be needed for
4 Oxygen bottles, medical kit, and other
5 Checklists ensure nothing
6 A security search ensures no suspicious

a equipment are safely stowed away.
b be carried on the flight.
c dangerous substances must be checked.
d gets missed from the routine procedures.
e troubleshooting if a fault occurs.
f items have been smuggled on board.

6 List items which the aircraft must carry on each flight. Which items must the aircraft not carry?

British English	American English
torch	flashlight

7 Find words in exercise 5 to match the meanings below.

1 finding and correcting a fault
2 items for emergency medical treatment
3 materials that cause harm
4 operations carried out regularly
5 packed/stored in a tidy way
6 brought secretly

Look again at the pictures in exercise 4. Answer the questions.

picture A   Why are these books carried on the flight?
picture B   When/how would the items in the picture be used?
picture C   What precautions are taken at airports to keep prohibited items off planes?
picture D   What documents may be carried on the flight?
picture E   Can you give an example of a load that requires a NOTOC?
picture F   In your experience, what problem found on a pre-flight check has delayed departure?

AUDIO
9

8   Listen to the two exchanges. Answer the questions.

1   Which one uses plain English? Which one uses standard phraseology?
2   Why is plain English used?

9   Choose the best ATC responses to complete each exchange.

Exchange 1

a   Sorry – you're totally unreadable.
b   Say again, calling.

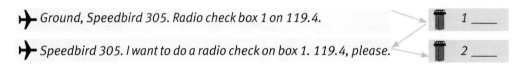

✈ Ground, Speedbird 305. Radio check box 1 on 119.4.   📢 1 ____

✈ Speedbird 305. I want to do a radio check on box 1. 119.4, please.   📢 2 ____

Exchange 2

a   Fedex 36, go ahead, sir.
b   Fedex 36 no, it's fine sir. You don't need any documents for Malaysia now.
c   Fedex 36, no sir. There's no special documentation needed.

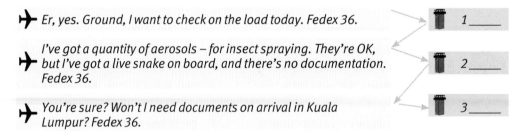

✈ Er, yes. Ground, I want to check on the load today. Fedex 36.   📢 1 ____

✈ I've got a quantity of aerosols – for insect spraying. They're OK, but I've got a live snake on board, and there's no documentation. Fedex 36.   📢 2 ____

✈ You're sure? Won't I need documents on arrival in Kuala Lumpur? Fedex 36.   📢 3 ____

Exchange 3

a   B344, my apologies. The computer has failed again and so that's obviously the reason.
b   OK, er, B344. I have your flight plan. Start up approved. The temperature is plus 17.
c   Sorry, B344. I've no flight plan for B344. Stand by. I'll check you out.
d   B344, stand by. I'll get back to you very shortly.

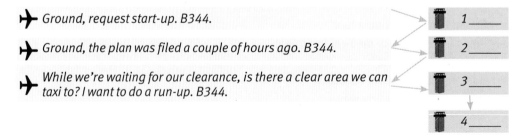

✈ Ground, request start-up. B344.   📢 1 ____

✈ Ground, the plan was filed a couple of hours ago. B344.   📢 2 ____

✈ While we're waiting for our clearance, is there a clear area we can taxi to? I want to do a run-up. B344.   📢 3 ____

📢 4 ____

AUDIO

10

Listen and check your answers. Then answer the questions.

1   In exchange 1, what problem does the pilot have?
2   In exchange 2, why was the pilot concerned?
3   In exchange 3, did the pilot file his flight plan on time?
    Why does he have to wait?

PRONUNCIATION

10 Put the words in the correct column.

cargo • control • unload • problem • something • pitot • delay

● ●	● ●
cargo	control

Listen and check your answers.

INTERACTIONS

11 Work with a partner. Look at the pictures. Ask ATC for a delay in start-up. Explain why.

USEFUL PHRASES

Asking for more time
Can we have more time?
Can we delay until 05?
We need 20 minutes.

Giving a reason
We have a problem with the cargo door.
There's something wrong with the conveyor belt.

Saying what you're going to do
We're going to try to fix it.
We're going to unload the plane.

1

2

3

You are a controller. Give advice to the pilot.

USEFUL PHRASES

Saying there's a problem
Speedbird 267, departure delayed until 25.
Cessna 945, check your pitot cover.
KE242, I can see a hatch open.

Requesting action
Can someone move the chocks, please?
Is someone going to clean that up?

4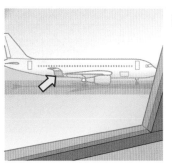

5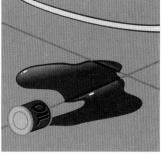

6

12 Work with a partner to practise an exchange between a transatlantic pilot and a controller.

PARTNER FILES ➤ Partner A File 2, p. 70
Partner B File 9, p. 72

COMPREHENSION

13 What items do you normally hear in an ATIS (Automatic Terminal Information Service) broadcast? Make a list.

AUDIO

12

14 Listen to the ATIS broadcast. Choose the correct answer to each question.

1	**What was the ATIS identifier letter?** a Z b S c H d R	**5**	**What was the QNH setting?** a 997 hPa b 987 hPa c 1027 hPa d 1007 hPa
2	**When was the message broadcast?** a 1510 b 1755 c 1515 d 1715	**6**	**Which was the departure runway?** a 22 left b 22 right c 23 left d 23 right
3	**What was the direction of the wind?** a 230 degrees b 160 degrees c 210 degrees d 260 degrees	**7**	**Which runway was closed?** a 29 b 28 c 18 d 19
4	**What height is the lowest cloud?** a 3500 feet b 2600 feet c 3900 feet d 2500 feet	**8**	**What local hazard was mentioned?** a Ice on runway b Workman close to runway c Birds in the area d Runway 22 closed

AUDIO

13

15 Listen to the ATIS broadcast. Complete the form.

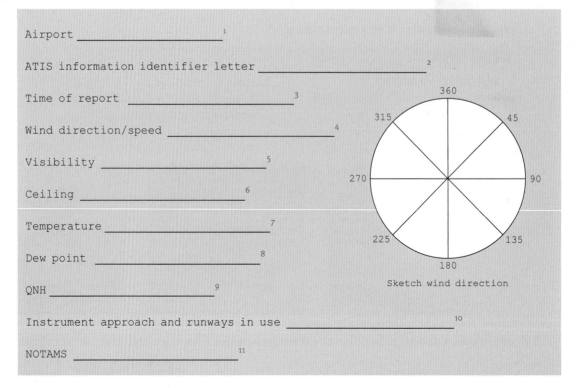

Airport _____ 1

ATIS information identifier letter _____ 2

Time of report _____ 3

Wind direction/speed _____ 4

Visibility _____ 5

Ceiling _____ 6

Temperature _____ 7

Dew point _____ 8

QNH _____ 9

Instrument approach and runways in use _____ 10

NOTAMS _____ 11

Sketch wind direction

VOCABULARY

16 Other broadcasts may contain more information on local conditions. Match the words to the pictures.

a   birds
b   CB clouds
c   earth tremors
d   hail
e   heavy rain
f   sandstorm
g   slush
h   snow drifts
i   strong winds
j   volcanic cloud

COMPREHENSION

AUDIO

14

17 Listen. Match each message to a picture above.

message 1 _____   message 3 _____   message 5 _____

message 2 _____   message 4 _____

Read the article and answer the questions.

My first long-haul flight was cancelled

As a flight attendant, I'd flown short haul many times, but this was my first long-haul flight. I was quite excited – so it was a bit of a shame that we never even got off the ground!

The captain had just started up – I went onto the flight deck for a minute, and as I opened the door, all the instruments were going crazy – flickering and flashing on and off. There was a funny noise, too. A sort of crackling sound. I didn't know what was going on, so I made a quick exit back to the cabin. Then, a few seconds later the smoke alarms went off. Nobody did anything at first – there was no smoke, so we just carried on getting everything ready for the safety announcements.

The chief steward went up to the flight deck though, and as soon as he opened the door, there was a sort of electrical burning smell. It was faint, but it was definitely something burning.

That's when it was obvious this wasn't a false alarm. The engines were shut down immediately. The chief steward came back and told us that both the ground crew and ATC had seen smoke coming from the plane.

The captain calmly taxied us back to a nearby stand and we got the passengers off as quickly as possible. It all worked really well. No one panicked. The fire service arrived straightaway and did a thorough check. Apparently they found quite a lot of damage from electrical arcing. We were very lucky that there hadn't been a fire.

OVER TO YOU

Name another safety feature which could prevent a minor incident becoming a disaster.
What is the manufacturer likely to do after this incident?
Have you heard of similar incidents on other aircraft?

3 Ground movements

STARTER

Look at the signals and signs. Where do you find them? Can you say what they mean?

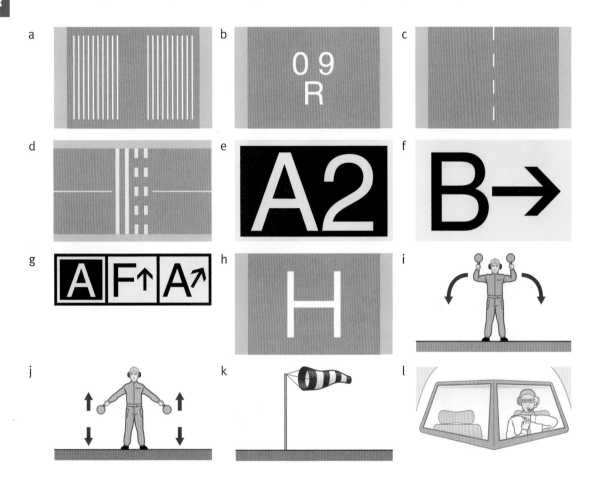

a   b   c

d   e   f

g   h   i

j   k   l

Match the signs and signals above with the names below.

1   centre line marking
2   runway taxi holding position
3   runway designator
4   taxiway location sign
5   direction sign
6   connect ground power

7   reserved for helicopter
8   move ahead
9   taxiway A changing direction
10 slow down
11 threshold markings
12 wind direction and speed

Now mark items 1–12 above with G (ground/surface marking), SN (sign) or SG (signal). Do you have any experience of signs or signals that were confusing or difficult to see? What was the problem?

1 Match each picture to a name and an action.

a

	Vehicle	Action
1	aircraft de-icer	transporting passengers
2	bus	spraying icy wings
3	fire engine	transporting construction materials
4	flat-bed truck	reversing planes
5	fuel tanker	repairing flat tyres
6	heavy plant	putting out fires
7	maintenance truck	getting rid of compacted ice
8	push-back tug	delivering kerosene
9	snowplough	clearing debris
10	sweeper	carrying cargo

b

c

d

e

f

g

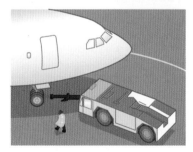

h

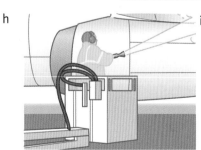

i

j

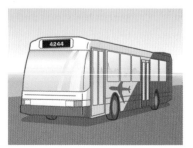

What is each vehicle used for? Use *is used for*.

A de-icer is used for spraying icy wings.

British English	American English
snowplough	snowplow
kerosene	jet fuel

AUDIO
15

2 **Listen. Where are the airside vehicles? Mark their locations.**

RYR 372 • fire tender • BA Bus 5 • sweeper • de-icer • RYR 355 • UAL 439 • maintenance truck

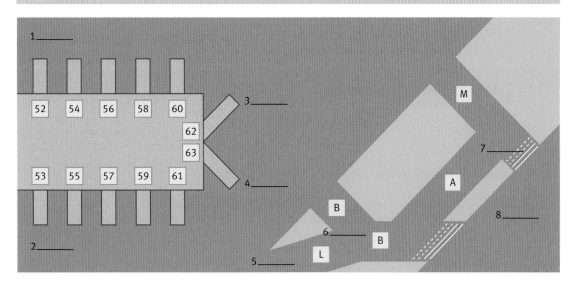

3 **Match the words and phrases for movement with the pictures.**

1	keep well to the left of	3	turn on to taxiway B	5	go straight ahead
2	backtrack	4	taxi off the runway	6	go beyond taxiway A

COMPREHENSION

4 **Match the sentence halves.**

1	I have to be near	a	due to works.
2	I have a flat tyre	b	on the nose gear.
3	Do you need	c	a radio problem.
4	I've got	d	a push-back tug?
5	A maintenance truck	e	our maintenance area.
6	Taxi with caution	f	is on its way for your flat.

AUDIO
16

Now listen and check your answers.

FLUENCY

5 **Listen again. Answer the questions or discuss them with a group.**

1 How many planes is ground control dealing with?
2 Describe the tug driver's difficulty.
3 What plane does KLM 219 give way to?
4 Why is the KLM pilot impatient?
5 What's the difference between *Taxi slowly* and *Taxi with caution*?

STRUCTURE

PERMISSION, OBLIGATION, PROHIBITION

Strong obligation: *have (got) to, must, mustn't,*
shall
Pilots **have to** *get clearance for flight plans.*
Passengers **mustn't** *carry fireworks on board.*
All passengers **shall** *pass through security.*

Recommendation: *should/ought to*
You **ought to** *slow down.*

No obligation: *don't have to, needn't*
Snowplough drivers **don't have to** *report to pilots.*

Permission: *may, can, are allowed to*
Request taxi. You **can** *route via taxiway.*
You **may** *proceed.*

Prohibition: *can't, don't*
You **can't** *start up.*
Don't *let the passengers enter the flight deck.*

6   **Complete the sentences with the words from the box.**

mustn't • should • have to • don't have to • are allowed to

1   Passengers _____ label their luggage clearly.
2   Passengers _____ carry compressed gases or other dangerous items on board.
3   Passengers _____ check in on the internet, but it's usually easier.
4   Passengers _____ take a small bag onto the plane with them.
5   Passengers _____ show their passports when they check in for an international flight.

7   **Ground movements are often expressed using phrasal verbs. Use the prepositions in the box to complete the phrasal verbs.**

off • on • up • down • back • around

1   Flight KLM 546, slow _____! You are taxiing too quickly.
2   My flat tyre made the steering unresponsive. I almost skidded _____ the runway.
3   Tug 4, you'll have to go _____ to stand 17 and assist SAS 418.
4   Ground Control Bus 4. Acknowledge stand change. Turn _____ and proceed to stand 13.
5   Gulf Alpha Bravo Lima, permission to carry _____ past the stationary 757.
6   China 412, pick up a little speed and catch _____ with the Airbus ahead of you.

AUDIO

17

PRONUNCIATION

8   **Listen. Underline the words that are stressed in each sentence.**

1   Can I <u>change</u> <u>stand</u>?
2   I have to be near our maintenance area
3   I have a flat tyre on the nose gear.
4   Hang on a minute.
5   Did you get my message?

Now listen again and check your answers.

9 **Which important words are stressed in these sentences?**

1 Taxi with caution due to works.
2 Hey, I can see lots of works.
3 Request closest available stand.
4 Is that possible?
5 I don't want to be difficult.

AUDIO
18

Listen and check your answers. Then practise the sentences with a partner. Make sure you use the correct intonation.

COMPREHENSION

AUDIO
19

10 **Controllers may give other essential information about local conditions. Listen to the audio and match the potential hazards to the numbered positions on the diagram.**

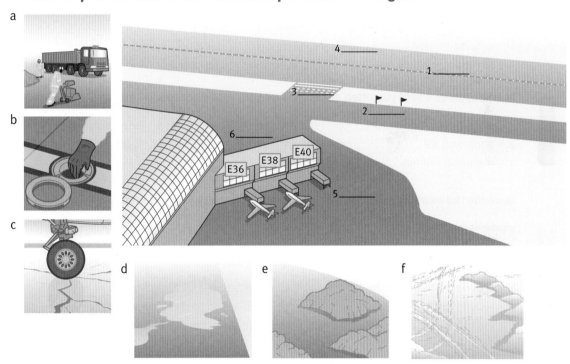

11 **Listen again and complete the sentences.**

1 Be informed. Centreline lights out of order _____ runway 27.
2 Caution. Construction work _____ the edge of the taxiway. It's marked by red flags.
3 Be advised. Ice reported _____ the holding area. Braking action poor. Caution.
4 Be advised. Standing water _____ the midpoint on the runway.
5 Caution. Slush _____ stand E40.
6 Be advised. Edge of apron partly covered _____ gravel opposite the terminal building.

INTERACTIONS

12 **Work with a partner to practise instructions.**

PARTNER FILES ➤ Partner A File 3, p. 70
Partner B File 11, p. 72

USEFUL PHRASES

There's some oil on the apron near stand D15.
Watch out for the dog near taxiway Alpha.
Be advised taxiway Charlie is partially flooded.

Suggest another taxiway.
Be advised of broken down truck ahead.
Request diversion, change of stand.

AUDIO
20

13 Bad weather may cause problems on the ground. Listen to Ground speaking to two pilots. Answer and discuss the questions.

1 Why is the Finnair flight taxiing with caution?
2 Why is the Singapore Airlines pilot impatient?
3 Has SIA 107 lost her slot time?
4 What is SIA 107's new slot time?

5 Does SIA 107 get approval for start-up?
6 Why does Finnair need to hold position?
7 What weather warnings are given?
8 What hazard is on the taxiway?

VOCABULARY

14 Match the words to describe weather conditions.

A
1 dense   thunderstorms
2 gusting   fog
3 severe   winds

B
1 flash   dust
2 broken   flooding
3 blowing   clouds

C
1 drifting   showers
2 scattered   storms
3 tropical   snow

In what places would you often expect to find these weather conditions?

1 widespread sandstorms
2 snow and ice
3 monsoon rainfall

4 hot dry summers
5 fog and drizzle
6 hurricanes

7 cool moist winters
8 typhoons

Describe the weather conditions at your own international airport in June and in December.

AUDIO
21

COMPREHENSION

15 Listen. Write T for true and F for false. Speedbird 937 ...

1 reports at holding point L4.
2 reports giving way to the Airbus 320.
3 is not prepared for immediate departure.

4 acknowledges holding at L3.
5 is asked to clear runway.
6 reports that the Airbus 320 has stopped on taxiway.

VOCABULARY

16 The Airbus 320 has stopped on the runway. Work with a partner to give as many reasons as possible why planes may stop.

1 Technical problem such as _____ .
2 Human factors such as _____ .
3 Weather conditions such as _____ .

4 Emergencies such as _____ .
5 Other causes such as _____ .

Put these problems in the categories above.

breakdown • fuel spillage • de-icing • malfunction • mechanical problems
• unruly passengers • engine failure • engine stall and surge • jammed doors
• being stuck in the mud • collisions • sick passengers • sick pilot • flash flooding
• heavy snowfall • poor visibility • engine on fire • police/customs control
• medical emergency • blocked runway • runway incursion • industrial action
• lost luggage • terrorism • animal on the runway

Have you experienced any of the situations in exercise 16?

17 Look at the pictures. Explain the problems to your partner.

1
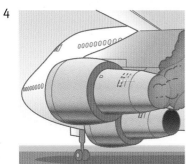

2

3

4

5

6

EXPLAINING PROBLEMS

There seems to be a problem with the door.	Engine number 2 has a malfunction.
We've got a problem with the service hatch.	There's a burst tyre.
Stand 6 seems to be blocked.	We've got a bit of a problem.
The cargo door appears to be stuck.	We may have a situation here.

COMPREHENSION

18 What happened to the Airbus 320? Complete this sentence with the exact words used by ground control.

Ground   The Airbus 320 is being towed off Runway 24 because of _____ .

INTERACTIONS

19 With a partner take the problems from your list in 16 on page 26 and use these phrases to say that the problem has been solved.

SAYING A PROBLEM HAS BEEN SOLVED

The delay/wait/problem is over.	It was a false alarm. We're back to normal.
It's been repaired.	The situation is under control.
The customs have finished their controls.	The Airbus problem seems to be over.
All clear.	It was nothing serious.
You've got the green light.	It's all over, let's get on.
Go ahead, all clear.	

20 Work with a partner to practise the exchange below. Take turns being the controller and the pilot.

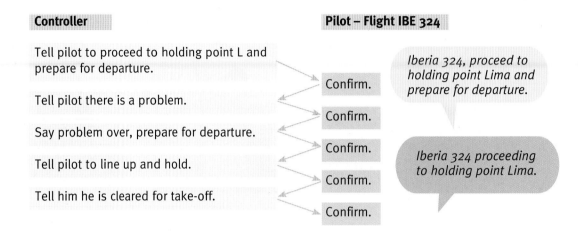

Controller	Pilot – Flight IBE 324
Tell pilot to proceed to holding point L and prepare for departure.	Iberia 324, proceed to holding point Lima and prepare for departure.
Confirm.	
Tell pilot there is a problem.	
Confirm.	
Say problem over, prepare for departure.	Iberia 324 proceeding to holding point Lima.
Confirm.	
Tell pilot to line up and hold.	
Confirm.	
Tell him he is cleared for take-off.	
Confirm.	

OUTPUT

Read the article and answer the questions.

Shortened runway exposes serious safety concerns

A Boeing 737-86N, with seven crew and 190 passengers on board, was beginning a flight. Runway 06L was in use but the flight crew were not aware that this runway was being operated at reduced length.

This was due to work-in-progress to remove rubber deposits at the far end of the runway, which was out of sight from the 06L threshold end as the runway is built over a slight rise in the ground. Due to a difference of interpretation of information passed between Air Traffic Control (ATC) and the flight crew, the aircraft entered the runway from holding point AG rather than the expected holding point A, and the takeoff was conducted using a reduced thrust setting calculated for the assumed normal runway length. As the aircraft passed the crest of the runway, the flight crew became aware of vehicles at its far end but, as they were now close to their rotation speed, they continued and carried out a normal takeoff. The aircraft passed within 56 feet of a 14-foot-high vehicle.

Notes
- A NOTAM was issued informing runway 06L works-in-progress.
- The co-pilot listened to the ATIS broadcast which contained details about the weather, bird activity, and the work-in-progress.
- Radio communications between ATC and the flight crew regarding the lining up point were misinterpreted by both parties.
- There were seven vehicles at the end of the runway.
- Work was in progress at the time of the incident.
- There was no blanking of runway lighting in the works-in-progress area.
- ATC advised the pilots about the reduced runway distance for take-off but taxi instructions did not give a specific holding point.
- The end of the runway was not visible at the threshold.
- The aircraft was travelling too fast to abort.
- The aircraft was 9 tonnes overweight for a reduced runway take-off.
- The pilots did not believe they had been in a serious incident and did not make a report.
- ATC witnessed the incident but it was not reported immediately.

OVER TO YOU

Do you think runway 06L should have been used?

Do you have experience of a similar situation?

What recommendations could be made based on this report?

4 Departure, climbing, and cruising

How many reasons can you think of for late departure? Make a list.

AUDIO
23

COMPREHENSION

1 **Listen to seven exchanges. Write the number of the exchange at the correct point on the diagram.**

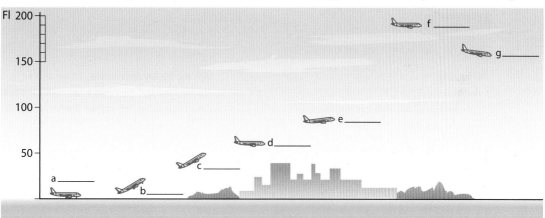

Listen again. Answer the questions.

exchange 1 Why didn't the pilot have the full runway length? Give two reasons.
exchange 2 What was the call sign of the aircraft?
exchange 3 How far out is the incoming traffic?
exchange 4 Was the aircraft instructed to turn right or left heading 090?
exchange 5 What is the standard radiotelephony phrase for *Just stay on the same heading for the time being?*
exchange 6 What heading is D6V given at the new level?
exchange 7 What was the wind speed?

Look at the transcripts on page 88. For each situation, think of what would be said next.
Use standard phraseology whenever possible.

2 **Match each incident or event from exercise 1 with a description.**

Incident/event		Description	
1	near collision	a	aircraft appears on radar screen
2	identified	b	avoiding manoeuvre appropriate
3	level bust	c	danger – aircraft are too close
4	airprox	d	aircraft doesn't become airborne
5	conflicting traffic	e	waiting or delaying
6	holding	f	traffic on collision course
7	aborted take off	g	over 300 feet outside assigned level

PRONUNCIATION

3 **Put the words in the correct column according to the underlined sound.**

> serv<u>ice</u> • <u>ch</u>ange • in<u>s</u>tead • wi<u>sh</u> • <u>ch</u>eck
> • <u>s</u>orry • <u>s</u>ay • <u>s</u>ure • approa<u>ch</u>

/s/	/ʃ/	/tʃ/
<u>s</u>ierra	<u>sh</u>ort	<u>ch</u>arlie

AUDIO

24

Listen and check your answers.

STRUCTURE

CHECKING AND ASKING FOR AN ALTERNATIVE

Checking	**Asking for an alternative**
Are you sure?	Do you mind if we have a level change **instead**?
Can you confirm climb back 120?	Can I use runway 9 **rather than** runway 18?
Did you say flight level 90?	

4 **Use words from the questions above to complete the sentences.**

1 _____ you say you checked the QNH setting?

2 _____ you sure you want us to use taxiway X?

3 Sorry, can we use runway 23 _____ of runway 28?

4 _____ you say you wanted medical assistance?

5 Can I change to FL 350 _____ than 310?

6 _____ you confirm you've reached FL 150?

AUDIO
25

Listen and check your answers. Which words are used for:

- an affirmative answer?
- a negative answer?

COMPREHENSION

5   **Look at the diagram. Listen to the exchange and complete the sentences from the second part of the exchange.**

Pilot	We have no visual with helicopter. Are you sure? L556.
Tower	Ah – L556, the helicopter is _____¹ the runway, sir.
Pilot	What? He's not even _____² the ground?
Co-pilot	Ah! I've got him. No conflict. Over there, look! He's hovering about 100 feet up, _____³ 3 o'clock. _____⁴ the airfield. _____⁵ the chimney. Just _____⁶ that large building.
Pilot	Where?
Co-pilot	Well _____⁷ to the right. _____⁸ the car park, _____⁹ the trees, _____¹⁰ the chimney. In fact if he gets any closer he'll bump _____¹¹ it! It's fine. No problem. He's well _____¹² our path.

6   **Answer the questions.**

1   Which words did the controller confuse?
2   Is this a language problem or an operational problem?

7 **Use eight prepositions from the box to complete the aircraft positions.**

PREPOSITIONS OF POSITION					
above	across	behind	next to	into	on
beyond	at	away	in front of	over	below

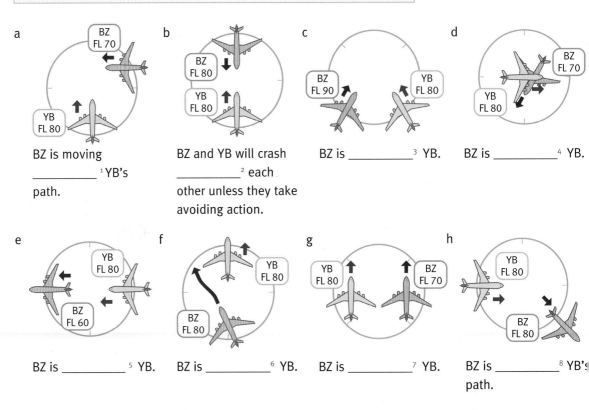

a BZ is moving _____ [1] YB's path.

b BZ and YB will crash _____ [2] each other unless they take avoiding action.

c BZ is _____ [3] YB.

d BZ is _____ [4] YB.

e BZ is _____ [5] YB.

f BZ is _____ [6] YB.

g BZ is _____ [7] YB.

h BZ is _____ [8] YB's path.

8 **Match each pair of aircraft (a–h) above to a description.**

1 _____ parallel
2 _____ converging
3 _____ opposite
4 _____ directly above/below

5 _____ diverging
6 _____ same direction
7 _____ overtaking
8 _____ crossing (right to left)

AUDIO
27

9 **Now listen. Write the letter of the diagram (a–h) above that matches each exchange.**

1 _____
2 _____
3 _____
4 _____

5 _____
6 _____
7 _____
8 _____

PRONUNCIATION

10 **Important words are stressed. Underline the important words in the sentences.**

1   Look out for slow-moving traffic 6 miles ahead.
2   Avoiding action. Turn left immediately, heading 125.
3   Opposite traffic at 12 o'clock.
4   Traffic to your left 2 miles. Overtaking FL 90.
5   Fast moving traffic at 2 o'clock crossing right to left.
6   Conflicting traffic at 6 o'clock.
7   Traffic 5 o'clock parallel. 1000 feet below, climbing.
8   Maintain FL 150 until further advised.
9   You're well clear of traffic.

AUDIO
28

Listen and check your answers.

INTERACTIONS

11 **Work with a partner. You are call sign YB. Listen to three warnings. For each situation mark both planes on the diagram. Ask your partner to repeat as many times as necessary.**

PARTNER FILES →   Partner A   File 4, p. 70
                  Partner B   File 10, p. 72

STRUCTURE

SAYING HOW MUCH	
Countable	**Uncountable**
There are **some** passengers boarding.	There's **some** ice on the runway.
There aren't **any** baggage trolleys.	There isn't **any** hail, just a little drizzle.
Are there **any** reports of wind shear?	Is there **any** fog?

12 **Complete the exchange using *some* and *any* in the correct places.**

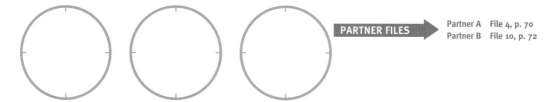

B550, we have a report of _____[1] vapour streaming aft of you.

Tumbiki Control, thanks. Sounds like we're losing _____[2] fuel. We're declaring an emergency. Returning to Tumbiki. B550.

B550, roger. Do you want to dump _____[3] fuel?

Affirmative. I'll have to get rid of _____[4]. I can't risk _____[5] overheating of the brake units. And I certainly don't want _____[6] fuel spilling onto hot brakes. B550.

B550, do you require _____[7] airport services?

Affirmative. I need _____[8] protection, please. Fire and rescue services required. B550.

AUDIO
29

Listen and check your answers.

INTERACTIONS

13 **Work with a partner. Use the chart to:**

- act as a pilot and pass useful information to ATC.
- act as an ATCO and give appropriate warnings to pilots.

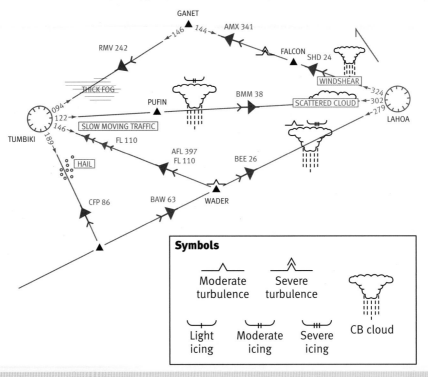

Symbols

⌃ Moderate turbulence	⋀ Severe turbulence
Light icing	Moderate icing	Severe icing	CB cloud

WARNINGS AND REQUESTS

Warnings

There's some clear air turbulence ahead.

There are a few scattered clouds.

There's a little icing reported at the higher level.

There isn't much fog at your destination.

Requests

How many other planes are in the area?

Is there lots of traffic ahead?

Is there a lot of bad weather ahead?

Are there any speed restrictions?

FLUENCY

14 **Read the first part of an account of an incident on take-off. What do you think caused the vibration?**

From the Flight Deck

Strange vibration on take-off

We taxied the short distance to runway 10. We received clearance immediately and started to roll. Before we reached 100 knots, everything was fine, but after 120 knots we felt some vibration on the flight deck. When the speed increased, the vibration increased. V1 was 140 knots so we took off and the vibration stopped as soon as we were airborne. The climb out was fine, but a warning light came on when we tried to retract the landing gear. We suspected a burst tyre and requested a runway inspection from ATC. While we waited for a reply, we discovered there was severe vibration in the middle and at the rear of the plane. Shortly afterwards, ATC told us there was tyre debris on the runway.

Read the rest of the account. Were you correct?

We declared a pan and decided to return to the airport as soon as possible. Once we were in the hold we remained there until we had burned enough fuel to give a safe landing weight. As soon as the plane touched down, the vibration started again on the flight deck. When we stopped, the fire service quickly surrounded the plane and foamed the landing gear. After braking, the temperature of the landing gear had risen to 800°C. Once the immediate danger was over, the passengers stayed on board until the plane was clear of the runway. When the crew disembarked, the damage to an outer tyre

was obvious. It was badly ripped. After investigation, tyre debris was found in number one engine. It had caused severe damage to 17 fan blades.

STRUCTURE

TIME EXPRESSIONS

When you're abeam HERON, you'll be clear of traffic.
As soon as I receive your flight plan, I'll give you your clearance.
We'll call you **once** he has vacated the runway.
We'll proceed to Birmingham **after** we pick up the additional cargo.
I'll call you **before** we reach the outer marker.
Continue your climb **until** you reach FL 270.
Wait there **while** I check the paperwork.

15 Choose the best time expression in each sentence from the account.

1 *Before/After/When* we reached 100 knots, everything was fine.
2 *While/Until/When* the speed increased, the vibration increased.
3 *After/While/Before* we waited for a reply, we discovered there was severe vibration in the middle, and at the rear of the plane.
4 *Before/Until/As soon as* the plane touched down, the vibration started again on the flight deck.
5 *After/While/Before* braking, the temperature of the landing gear had risen to 800°C.
6 *Once/Until/Before* the immediate danger was over, the passengers stayed on board *while/as soon as/until* the plane was clear of the runway.

16 **With a partner or small group, discuss the questions.**

1   Suggest other incidents which may cause vibration on the flight deck or in the cabin.
2   What other damage may be caused by a tyre burst?
3   Why do you think there was vibration in the centre and rear of the plane?
4   Describe another incident where a plane returned to the airport shortly after take off. Give reasons for the return.

GIVING REASONS

The plane returned **because of** a fuel leak.
The plane remained in the hold **in order to** reduce its landing weight.
The damage was **due to** a bird strike.

OUTPUT

Read the news article and the technical report. Then answer the questions.

Flying enthusiast's dream shattered

Flying enthusiast Max Wright thought he had achieved his dream. After years of careful work, he completed a self-build LAC-02 Falcon light aircraft kit.

A few practice hours later, Wright was ready for the first flight, with his friend Will Strong as his first passenger. He carefully carried out all the pre-flight checks. Everything was in A1 condition.

Lining up for take off, the electric fuel pump was switched to ON and the roll out was perfect.

Then it all went wrong. At approximately 150–200 feet, the engine coughed and stopped suddenly.

Onlookers said they heard the engine falter and looked up to see the plane banking sharply to the left. The aircraft was losing height rapidly, but somehow Wright managed to land it safely. Both the pilot and his passenger escaped with only minor cuts on their hands after the heavy landing.

Wright decided the plane should be repaired by the kit manufacturers. He has requested an investigation into the reason for the engine failure.

FLITE-KITS LIMITED

TECHNICAL REPORT

Aircraft type: LAC-02 Falcon

Engine type: Piston engine

Engineer's report
A piece of heat resistant material from the engine compartment was obstructing the fuel flow to the carburettors. This material must have got in when the engine was built as it was downstream of the filter which fuel passes through after leaving the fuel tank. It seems it was gradually carried along the fuel pipes until it reached the carburettors, where it blocked them completely.

OVER TO YOU

What would your reaction be if this was your aircraft?
What responsibilities do aircraft kit manufacturers have to their customers?
What light aircraft have you flown in?
Would you like to build a light aircraft?

5 En route events

How many of the activities or hazards can you name?

What other hazards might be met during a flight?

COMPREHENSION

1 **Listen to the navigation warnings. Match each warning to an activity.**

warning 1	a	fuel dumping
warning 2	b	in-flight refuelling
warning 3	c	warning light inoperable
warning 4	d	weather balloon
warning 5	e	fireworks display

Which of these hazards are not pictured in STARTER, above?

2　Listen again if necessary and answer the questions.

1　Where is the weather balloon?
2　What is the problem at Marchwood?
3　What is happening at FL 100?
4　What will finish at 1500?
5　How long will the display last?

3　NOTAMs give information about operational situations. After initial details of location, times, and dates, the message is a shortened form of plain English. Can you read this message?

> B) 08/05/04 11:45 UTC C) 08/05/06 17:30
> AIR DISPLAY AND ASSOCIATED INTENSE AERIAL ACTIVITY INCL JET AND PROP ACFT PLUS HEL. NO ACFT IS TO FLY WI AREA OF A CIRCLE RAD 3.5 NMS CENTRED AT 5205N 00008E UNLESS APPROVED BY ATC. PILOTS TO EXER CTN IN THE VCY. OPS INFO CONTACT 07780-870-476.

With a partner, translate the message into plain English.

AUDIO
31

4　Listen to the navigation warnings. Complete the table to show any traffic restrictions at the times shown. Write *yes* or *no*.

		Activity	1000	1200	1400	1600
1	Merthyr					
2	Land's End					
3	Brecon Beacons					
4	Bath					
5	Hatfield					

5　Put the words into the correct column according to the sound of the vowel (a, e, i, o, u).

testing • hang • laser • parachute • zero • training • balloon • demolition • explosives • display • fighters • flight • jumping • gliding • dumping • until • downwind • delay • controlled • avoid

/ə/	/ʌ/	/ɪ/	/e/	/æ/	/eɪ/	/əʊ/	/aɪ/
around	run	hit	best	bad	take	go	right
		testing					

AUDIO
32

Listen and check your answers.

INTERACTIONS

6 **Work with a partner. Translate a NOTAM into plain English for your partner. Then listen to your partner's NOTAM. Record the information.**

Start + finish times _____

Place _____

Activity _____

Additional information _____

PARTNER FILES ▶ Partner A   File 5, p. 71
Partner B   File 12, p. 72

> **USEFUL PHRASES**
>
> This information is for the 8th of May 2004.
> It is valid from 0800 to 1100 UTC.
> Aeroplanes flying in Devon and Cornwall should be aware of fighter training and parachute jumping.

STRUCTURE

AUDIO
33

7 **Advance information is not always available for unusual events. Listen to the three exchanges. Complete the sentences below.**

1   a   333 wants _____ separation.
    b   The pilot wants a _____ _____ ride.
    c   ATC says to expect _____ climb at 45.
2   a   The pilot says it's the _____ climb out ever.
    b   Then he says that the situation is _____ _____ than he thought.
3   a   AF-39 requests diversion to the _____ airport.
    b   The smell is getting _____ .

Listen again and check your answers.

8 **Compare the aeroplanes in the pictures with a partner. Use the words from the box to help you. Add your own ideas.**

short • long • heavy • new • old • big • roomy • fast • fuel efficient • advanced

INTERACTIONS

COMPARING TWO THINGS
The runway at Heathrow is **longer than** at Southampton. I have a **more expeditious** routing for you. The visibility is **better** here than in Athens. The weather is **worse** than before.

COMPARING MORE THAN TWO THINGS
Cirrus is **the highest** of all tropospheric clouds. Safety is **the most important** aspect of aviation. **The best** thing about flying is the speed of travel. That was **the worst** turbulence I've ever felt.

9 The unusual events in exercise 7 may or may not be life threatening. Answer the questions.

1 Which event is more likely to become life threatening?
2 Which event is less likely to become life threatening?
3 Which event is likely to lead to a mayday or pan-pan call?

Discuss with a partner and put all three events in the most appropriate column below.

MINOR		SERIOUS EMERGENCY	
Unlikely to get worse	May get worse	May become life threatening	Life threatening now

Add these events to the most appropriate column in the above table.

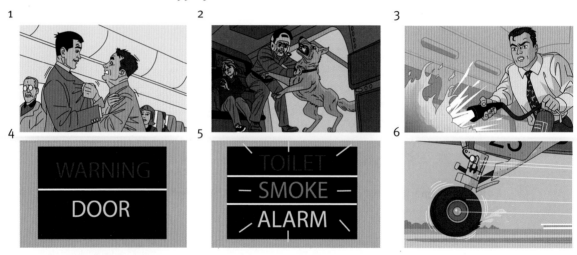

1
2
3
4 WARNING DOOR
5 TOILET – SMOKE – ALARM
6

What other events can you add to the columns in the table?

TALKING ABOUT PROBABILITY				
0%		50%		100%
↑ definitely won't	↑ probably won't /is unlikely to	↑ may/ might (not)	↑ will probably /is likely to	↑ will definitely

You **definitely won't** find standard phraseology for every emergency.
We **probably won't** be ready on time. Can we have another slot, please?
You are **unlikely to** see nimbostratus clouds from the ground.
Significant icing **may/might** jam the controls.
A warning light on the flight deck **may not/might not** be serious.
You **will probably** need to use plain English in an unusual situation.
Subsidence inversions **are likely to** be found beneath high pressure systems.
Severe icing **will definitely** reduce lift and increase drag.

10 Test your aviation awareness. Choose the best word to complete the sentences in the quiz.

1 If an aircraft suffers engine failure on take-off, it _____ climb more slowly than expected.
a is unlikely to   b is likely to   c probably won't

2 An unexplained loss of communications and a change in direction of flight _____ indicate unlawful interference of the aircraft, such as a hijack.
a definitely won't   b may   c definitely will

3 An overflight or clearance refusal is inconvenient but _____ become a major problem.
a will probably   b will definitely   c is unlikely to

4 After a sudden loss of pressurisation at altitude the crew _____ descend to a lower altitude.
a definitely won't   b might   c will definitely

5 An aircraft landing heavy _____ land more slowly than normal.
a definitely won't   b is likely to   c will definitely

6 If an aircraft has a problem with the landing gear on approach, it _____ go around.
a is likely to   b is unlikely to   c probably won't

7 An aborted take-off at high speed _____ increase the temperature of the brakes and might cause a fire.
a will probably   b might   c will definitely

8 If a crew are suffering from hypoxia, they _____ read back instructions incorrectly.
a probably won't   b may   c are unlikely to

9 Medical problems such as nose bleeds and burst ear drums _____ occur after a sudden loss of pressure.
a are unlikely to   b will definitely   c will probably

10 Increased noise during an emergency _____ make communications more difficult.
a might   b probably won't   c definitely won't

11 Think again about the situations in exercise 7. For each situation discuss with a partner what might happen next. Use the words in TALKING ABOUT PROBABILITY on page 40.

COMPREHENSION

12 **Listen to what happened next and answer the questions below.**

1   a   Was there a smoother ride at the higher level?
    b   What separation does the pilot ask for?
2   a   What went wrong?
    b   Which runway does the pilot choose?
3   a   What reason for the smell does the pilot suggest?
    b   Does the fire service board the plane before or after the passengers disembark?

Listen again and check your answers.

13 **There may be medical problems during flights. Approximately 75 per cent of in-flight medical emergencies are managed by the cabin crew. Others may require help from a doctor on the ground. Match the descriptions at the top of page 43 with the pictures below.**

1   He's having chest pains.
2   She's fainted.
3   He's having stomach pains.
4   She may be going into labour.
5   He's got asthma.

6   She's having a seizure.
7   He's hurt his head.
8   She's cut her hand.
9   He's behaving very aggressively.
10 He's choking.

AUDIO
35

14 Listen. Match each exchange to a picture on page 42.

1 _____   2 _____   3 _____   4 _____   5 _____   6 _____

FLUENCY

15 Read the first part of the story. Answer the questions.

Flying Lesson Takes Unexpected Turn

Matt Lewis was overjoyed when he took off in a light plane for his first flying lesson. However, the flight turned out to be more eventful than expected.

The flight began smoothly. The instructor, Ian McLean, took the controls for departure, and after acknowledging ATC instructions, handed the controls to Lewis. Flying a level course, Lewis was surprised when McLean started to test his new student's flying skills so early in the lesson. McLean flung himself backwards in his seat and then slumped forwards onto the controls. "I thought it was part of the lesson, or maybe a joke. I thought he wanted to see what I'd do if I really had to fly the plane." Lewis pulled McLean off the controls and continued straight ahead. "When ATC came on the radio to ask why we were off course, and McLean didn't answer, I knew it wasn't a joke."

1   What did Lewis think McLean was doing?
2   How will Lewis explain to ATC what has happened to his instructor?
3   What do you think happened next?

Read the second part of the story. Were you right?

Lewis told ATC that McLean had passed out after some sort of seizure, and that he was a student pilot on his first flight. ATC assigned a mayday status, and within minutes a second instructor, Nico Gamalev, was alongside Lewis in another aircraft. Together, they turned back to the airfield, and the new instructor talked Lewis through bringing the plane down safely.

McLean is now recovering in hospital and Lewis has declared that he's ready for his next flying lesson – with Mr Gamalev.

16 Read the statement from ICAO. Answer the question.

Incapacitation of the flight crew will normally require an automatic landing on suitably equipped aircraft. However, on passenger aircraft locked cockpit doors which can only be opened from the flight deck have sparked criticism.

Aircraft security is essential. The well-being of the flight crew is equally important.
How well are these two requirements balanced on commercial flights?

Read the article and answer the questions.

Eyewitness account of United flight 811

The flight left late at night. I was in a window seat in the middle of the plane. The weather was good and the take-off and climb out were fine. About 20 minutes into the flight there was a slight vibration. It was odd. Then, about 30 seconds later there was a loud noise – a bang – and then there was a big, big rush of air. The cabin filled with fog. It was fogged up for about 15 seconds.

It was a terrible mess. Papers and loose items were flying everywhere. The noise was really loud. The oxygen masks dropped down, and the temperature in the cabin reached freezing in about five seconds! And then I saw that there was a hole in the side of the plane! I was lucky: it was on the opposite side of the aircraft from me.

At first, the cabin crew just hung on. They were trying to understand what had happened. The noise made it impossible to communicate. It was night, so it was impossible to know how high we were. Then the crew started to move passengers away from the hole. Four of us helped to move them towards the rear of the plane. Once they were out of danger we strapped ourselves back in to our seats.

Time passed very slowly. It felt like hours before I looked out the window and saw lights. But really, it was only about 20 minutes after the incident. Two minutes later the intercom came on. The pilot said that we would be landing in two minutes. We landed within the two minutes and the landing was one of the smoothest I have ever had in a 747!

OVER TO YOU

Can you explain in your own words what happens during an explosive decompression?
What features on a modern aircraft are designed to make an explosive decompression very unlikely?
What other safety features have you heard of that aircraft manufacturers are working on at the moment?

6 Contact and approach

Read the pilot-to-passenger announcements. Grade them according to your preference (1 is the best, 3 is the worst). Give reasons for your choices and compare them with a partner.

> *From the flight deck, we're inbound on long final, approximately 22 minutes from our ETA of 1742 hours local. Weather conditions good, with scattered clouds at 5000 feet. Prepare for landing.*

> *Good afternoon, ladies and gentlemen, this is the first officer. We'll be landing in Shanghai in approximately 20 minutes. The temperature in Shanghai is a warm 28 degrees and the local time is now 5:20 in the evening. We hope you've enjoyed your flight.*

> *Hi, there. Captain here. In fact we're getting ready to land just now – we'll be down on that ground in a short while. It's a great day down there, just the sort of day I like. I love the food here, too. A lot better than we've had on this flight, hey. We'll see you on the ground.*

With a partner, list some 'rules' for good pilot-to-passenger communication. Think about:

- local information
- technical information and use of jargon
- courtesy
- clarity
- humour

COMPREHENSION

1   Listen. Answer the questions.

Part 1

1   What is the situation with flight 276?
2   What caused problems at the airport earlier in the day?
3   When does 276 need to land?
4   What's the reason for the landing time?
5   What is the expected delay?

Part 2

1   How long does Approach say 276 will need to wait?
2   What flight level change does 276 make?

Part 3

1   What does ATC instruct 276 to do?
2   Why can't 276 land at Wessex?

STRUCTURE

2   Read the sentences from the exchange. Are they talking about *when* or *how long?* Write W for *when*. Write H for *how long*.

1   _____   We had delays earlier today.
2   _____   It took a long time to clear it all.
3   _____   So how long can I expect to wait?
4   _____   I need to get down before 2300, don't I?
5   _____   Delays will be about half an hour, at least.
6   _____   I'll get back to you shortly.
7   _____   Climb immediately to 9000 feet.

3   Match each question with an answer.

1	When was the flight due to arrive?	a	About two months.
2	How much longer will we be holding?	b	We left ages ago!
3	How long did you spend in Asia?	c	An hour ago, so it's quite late.
4	When will we arrive?	d	For a few minutes more.
5	When did you leave Tokyo?	e	In about an hour.
6	How long will the backlog take to clear?	f	It might take over an hour.

TALKING ABOUT TIME		
The past	**The future**	**How long (duration)**
just now	immediately	a few seconds
a few minutes ago	shortly/ soon	not long
a while ago	in a few minutes/a while	a few minutes
this morning	in a few hours	a couple of hours
yesterday	tomorrow	quite a while
last week	next week	a long time
a long time ago	a long time from now	days
ages ago	ages from now	ages

4 Work with a partner. Use *ago* to say when each weather condition happened. Use *took* or *lasted* to say the duration. It is now noon on Tuesday.

Friday	Saturday	Sunday	Monday	Tuesday
1000–2400	0200–0800	0600–0830	1145–1600	0800–1200

Now talk about your own future. What are you going to do in a few minutes? In a few hours? A long time from now?

5 Listen to the announcement. Complete the sentences below.

1 I _____ for the delay this evening.
2 I'm _____ there are severe delays at Wessex due to air traffic.
3 Wessex has got a noise abatement curfew, so we _____ _____ after 11 p.m.
4 We've been _____ to Exeter.
5 Please accept our sincere _____ for the inconvenience.
6 We _____ this will mess up a lot of your plans.
7 The cabin crew will _____ to look after you until we reach Exeter.
8 Ground staff in Exeter will be _____ to make sure you reach your final destination as soon as possible.

Which sentences:

Apologise? Explain the problem? Offer a solution?

EXPLAINING CHANGES IN PLANS	
Apologizing I'm really sorry about the delay. I apologize for making you wait.	**Explaining the problem** The airport is covered in dense fog. We've had some trouble with the computer.
Offering a solution We'll hold a while longer. I can sort things out for you now.	

Think of a problem you have experienced. Answer the questions.

1 How was the problem explained?
2 What apology was offered?
3 What solution was offered?

TALKING ABOUT CAUSE AND EFFECT

If the snow **is** heavy, the airport **will close**.
If you **miss** your approach, you **will have to** go around.
If it **gets** too late, you**'ll have to** land at your alternate airport.

6   **Look at the approach plate on page 49. Match the sentence halves.**

1 If plane c is the fastest,	a it will be number 4 or 5 to land.
2 If plane a continues on its heading,	b it will slow down.
3 If plane e joins the circuit,	c it will fly over the airport and turn right.
4 If plane d wants to increase separation from plane b,	d it will come too close to plane 4.
5 If plane b speeds up,	e it will be the first on the ground.
6 If plane f enters the pattern,	f it will lead to a missed approach.

7   **Use information from the chart on page 49 to talk about cause and effect. Try to make five sentences.**

If you tune your radio to 127.3, you'll hear the LED ATIS.

38

8   **Listen. Write the flight number for each plane marked on the approach plate on page 49.**

AFL 339 • AUA 26 • DLH 1390 • BAW 440 • AZA 29 • BAW 34

plane a _____   plane d _____
plane b _____   plane e _____
plane c _____   plane f _____

9   **Flight KLM 405 is on approach for St Petersburg. Listen. Complete the table.**

Altitude: _____ 1
KE time: _____ 2
Estimated OLSON: _____ 3
Flight level to descend to: _____ 4
QNH: _____ 5
Speed: _____ 6 reducing to _____ 7

Discuss these questions with a partner.

What unit of altitude measurement is used at your local airport?
Have you ever worked with a different altitude measurement?
What other measurements can be expressed in different units?

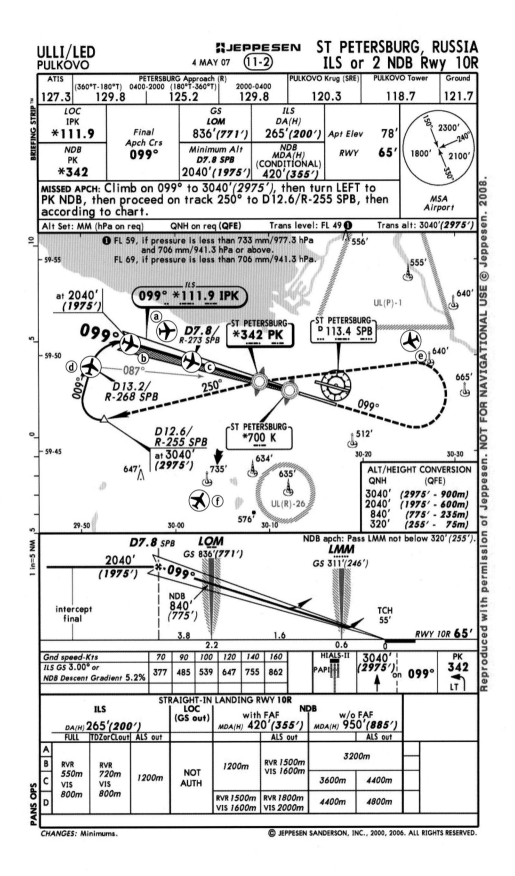

AUDIO

40

COMPREHENSION

10 Listen to the Flight Information Service (FIS) broadcast and note the nine pieces of information.

1   *Information Romeo* _____   6 _____

2 _____   7 _____

3 _____   8 _____

4 _____   9 _____

5 _____

Were any of the words difficult to understand?

AUDIO
41

PRONUNCIATION

11 Now listen to a different version of the same broadcast and check your answers.

With a partner, take turns reading the FIS broadcast.

> Information Romeo: 2000 Z, 8000 scattered, visibility 14 kilometres, temperature 44, wind 310, 8 knots, altimeter 30.00, expect ILS or visual to runway 24 and 33, advise on first contact you have information Romeo.

FLUENCY

12 Read the text. Why do you think the gear was up?

> On a clear July day, Scott Dittamo was training at the Newark Tower when he spotted an Air India flight with 409 passengers on board making its final approach. But something didn't look right. The Boeing 747's landing gear was still up as the plane was a half mile from landing.
>
> *ATC*   Air India 145 heavy, check gear down, gear appears up.
> *Pilot* Wow! Roger. Got it. Nice timing. Air India 145.
>
> The plane landed safely.

Do you know any similar stories of 'near-miss' situations?

13 Pilots with landing gear problems sometimes have to go around. Give other reasons for a missed approach.

AUDIO

42

Listen. Answer the questions.

1   What speed does KLM 405 reduce to?
2   What's the condition of the runway?
3   Why does KLM 405 decide to go around?

AUDIO
43

14 **KLM 405 is again on approach. Listen and answer the questions.**

1   What does the pilot ask about?
2   What does Approach say?

15 **Match the phrases (1–4) with the descriptions (a–d).**

1   What's the situation with ... ?   a   a piece of advice
2   No better, no worse.   b   a description of the situation
3   Be sure to check ...   c   a statement that means *the same as before*
4   There's slight aquaplaning reported.   d   a request for information

AUDIO
44

16 **Listen to another approach exchange. Answer the questions.**

1   Why does Approach say *Hang on*?
2   Why does Approach ask AA 745 to use runway 24?
3   Which direction does the pilot take for runway 24?
4   Approach says *Do you mind ... ?* What does this mean?
     a *Attention please!*   b *Is it OK?*   c *Take care.*
5   The pilot says *No problem*. What does this mean?
     a *Yes.*   b *What's the problem?*   c *No, there's a problem.*

STRUCTURE

> **REQUESTS**
>
> There is standard phraseology for making requests. However you frequently hear plain English.
> **Can** *you increase your speed?*
> **Hang on ... do you mind** *going for runway 24?*
> **Would you** *organize an ambulance on arrival?*
> **Could I ask you** *for the latest met reports in Tokyo?*

INTERACTIONS

17 **Work with a partner. Practise making requests.**

USEFUL LANGUAGE	
Saying yes	**Saying no**
No problem.	Sorry, I can't do that. It's broken.
Yes, of course.	I'm afraid not. I don't have the key.
Sure.	Sorry, that won't be possible. I don't know how.

PARTNER FILES   Partner A   File 7, p. 71
Partner B   File 13, p. 73

AUDIO
45

18 **Listen to another approach exchange. WHF-22 has just been cleared to base leg by Newbury Tower. Listen. Answer the questions.**

1   What altitude was the plane cleared to on base leg?
2   Why didn't the crew know they were too low?
3   What was the tower's main concern with the level bust?
4   Do you think this was a language problem or an operational problem?

Read the article and answer the questions.

SAFETY SENSE

Advice from the CAA of the United Kingdom

Correct standard phraseology is extremely important and must be used whenever possible. If it isn't used, the results can be devastating.

Precise phraseology is there for a reason – use it!
The aircraft was at 2400 feet. The controller gave clearance to *Descend two four zero zero cleared for approach*. The pilot thought the instruction was *Descend to four zero zero* and replied *OK, four zero zero*.

The controller did not notice the error.

It was night. There was no radar. Less than a minute later the aircraft crashed into a hillside at 437 feet.

> **REMEMBER**
> In the UK, climb and descent instructions always use the words flight level, altitude, or height.
>
> Say *Climb to … or Descend to … altitude or height.*
>
> Say *Climb flight level … (not Climb to flight level …)*

Listen and check for read-back.
The ATC instruction was given *Re-clear to three thousand feet expect an ILS approach. Report level three thousand feet.*

The pilot read back *Re-cleared to two thousand feet.* The controller did not hear, or ask for, any read-back from the pilot.

In addition, the QNH was set incorrectly, so when the altimeter indicated 2000 feet, the plane was actually at 1800 feet. The plane crashed into a mountainside, only 100 feet below the summit at 1795 feet.

> **REMEMBER**
> If you are in any doubt about a transmission, or do not receive the expected read-back, then check.

Use correct wording. Make urgent instructions sound urgent.

An inbound Airbus 320 was descending to FL 90. At the same time, a Boeing 757 was climbing to 6000 feet.

To maintain safe separation ATC told the 757 to *Head one hundred degrees and climb flight level eight zero*.

The pilot read back *One zero zero and flight level eight zero*, but the co-pilot set the autopilot incorrectly at flight level 100.

ATC saw the 757 climb above flight level 80. He told the pilot to stay at FL 80 and the pilot replied *We were cleared climb one zero zero*.

ATC told the 757 to stop climbing at FL 90 and told the A320 to stop descending at FL 100.

However, the controller did not say *avoiding action* so the pilots did not understand the instructions were urgent. As a result they responded slowly and the A320 reached flight level 93 before it stopped descending.

An accident was avoided, but the aircraft passed each other with 1 NM horizontal separation and only 300 feet vertical separation.

> **REMEMBER**
> In the UK, say *flight level one hundred* but *heading one zero zero*.
>
> Always give clear instructions and check the read-back!

Are the above recommendations the same as or different from ICAO recommendations?

Do you know of a serious incident which resulted from bad communication?

Why can *Go ahead* cause confusion?

As a controller, do you listen to read-back? As a pilot, do you always give read-back?

7 Landing

STARTER

Look at three exchanges. Which is the best? Which is the worst? Why?

1 Flight 402

ATC 402, descend on the glide path. Number two behind a 737 six miles ahead.

Pilot 402 descend on the glide path number two behind a 747 six miles ahead.

ATC 737, 402.

Pilot Approach, she's definitely a heavy. We've got a clear view. 402.

ATC Roger, 747. Pick up a bit of speed 402.

Pilot What would you like? 402.

ATC Er, 402, increase to 200 knots to the outer marker then reduce to 180. Report on final.

Pilot 402 increasing to 200 knots to outer, then 180 report on final . By the way, she's a heavy for sure.

ATC OK, got you, 402.

Pilot Approach, 402 on final. Speed 180.

ATC 402, number one to land reduce to 150 cleared for straight-in.

Pilot Cleared for straight-in. 402.

2 10

Pilot Outer marker. 10.

ATC Continue approach for runway 25R. Be advised the high intensity lights are on.

Pilot 10 final, we have the runway in sight.

ATC Cleared to land, wind 230 12 knots.

Pilot Cleared to land, wind 230 12 knots. Tell them to turn down the lights, they're far too bright.

ATC Too light confirm.

Pilot Er ... affirmative, too bright. Dim the lights, please.

ATC Wilco. Cleared to land 10.

3 Foxtrot 312 Heavy

Pilot Approach, Foxtrot 312 heavy, this is the fourth time I've circled in the stack. Any news?

ATC Stand by, Foxtrot 312 heavy.

Pilot Request diversion to Colorado Springs. 312.

ATC Stand by, Foxtrot 312.

Time interval

ATC OK 312, what can I do for you?

Pilot I need to know what's going on up here. We're all running out of patience and maybe fuel.

ATC Foxtrot 312, did you request a diversion to Colorado Springs?

Pilot Hey, I wasn't serious. Get me down on the ground please. 312.

ATC Foxtrot 312, descend to altitude 60, wind 250 degrees 14 knots You're number three. Report on short final.

Pilot Got it, descend to 60, wind 250, 14. Get back to you on final. Foxtrot 312.

Foxtrot 312 Heavy says *Hey, I wasn't serious*. Do you often hear jokes on frequency?

1 Look at these news reports on landing incidents. Match each headline with part of an article below.

a Airliner Belly-Flops on Blenheim Landing

b *Heavy Rains Close Runways*

c Plane Lands with Landing Gear Retracted

d **Nine Landing Jets Skid Off Runway in Three Months**

e Landing Only Delayed but Could Have Been Worse

f **Emergency Landing for JetStar in Three Week Old A330**

g **Pilots to Undergo Training for Short Runway Landings**

1 _____

A Monarch Airlines flight was on Friday delayed in landing after the emergency communications system and all the landing lights at the airfield failed, according to sources close to the airfield.

2 _____

According to a study reported in this paper, there were nine incidents in the last three months where passenger jets skidded off wet runways after landing at various airports.

3 _____

The Civil Aviation Authority is investigating why a second airliner flight landing in Blenheim had problems with its landing gear in the space of a month. On June 18, a similar type aircraft flight belly-flopped on the runway after its landing gear failed to lower. All passengers were unhurt. The plane was still in a hangar being repaired on Friday.

4 _____

The pilot did an inflight shutdown of the left-hand engine and landed the almost-new plane without incident. The aircraft has the capability of flying with one engine. It has a very experienced captain and crew on board. There was a fault found and he followed process to the letter and went to the nearest international airport.

5 _____

What do you do if you are the pilot of a passenger jet that has to land in the middle of a monsoon downpour? During rains, when visibility drops below the permissible limit, no pilot is allowed to land. Air traffic control (ATC) tells them when the water level on the runway falls below the 3 mm benchmark. But that's about all the information they get. Levels of water 'contamination' are rarely reported.

6 _____

Rio's Santos Dumont has a runway of just 1,323 metres so pilots are required to undergo extra familiarization at the airport to ensure that they put the aircraft down precisely at the right speed to stop within the published figures.

7 _____

As reported earlier, the aircraft was not configured to land. The landing gear was up and the flaps, normally down for landing, were retracted.

How often do you read about aviation incidents in the newspaper? Do you think newspapers cover aviation clearly, fairly, and accurately?

REPORTED SPEECH

When we talk about things that other people have said, we usually use *said that* or *says that* and the simple past tense.
The newspaper **said that** the plane had a 'soft landing', but a landing with gear up is never soft!

When a small plane is lost, the news always **says that** the pilot didn't file a flight plan. But they never say that pilots of light planes often don't file a flight plan!

VOCABULARY

2 **Complete these sentences using the words and phrases highlighted in the articles.**

1 In the tropics, a _____ often hinders pilots from landing.

2 The cargo plane with jammed gear _____ on the runway.

3 Flaps should not be _____ for landing.

4 The experienced flight engineer _____ and soon solved the technical fault.

5 Debris is the most common cause of _____ on a runway.

6 In such slippery conditions, the A320 _____ the runway at excessive speed.

7 _____ with certain airfields is obviously vital for safety.

AUDIO
46

3 Put the words in the correct column according to their stress patterns.

skidding • inadequate • hangar • landing gear • belly-flopped • configured
• downpour • slippery • information • retracted • reported • incident

● ●	● ● ●	● ● ●	● ● ● ●	● ● ● ●

Listen and check your answers.

4 Read the first part of the incident report. Do you have any experience with a similar situation? What happened?

> **Incident Report**
> The crew of SAS 105 received a call from ATC to advise them that airport staff had seen a wheel fall off the plane on take-off. ATC had contacted the company and they suggested the crew ought to divert to the alternate where maintenance facilities were better than at their destination. As it was only a short flight ATC thought they should continue to their destination because the weather at the alternate was very bad and the light was fading fast. In any event the plane would need time to burn off fuel and make preparations for landing. The company agreed that a daylight landing would be preferable and offered to help the crew with any decisions regarding the landing configuration at the destination.

AUDIO
47

5 Listen and complete the audio exchange.

Pilot   There's no ECAM message so _____ _____¹ you check the handbook now, so we can work out how to get this thing down safely.

ATC   _____² you _____³ me to put you through to your company?

Co-pilot   Possibly – _____⁴ you _____⁵ give me a few minutes to check the handbook and then call back?

ATC   Roger. _____⁶ call you back in two minutes, _____⁷ I?

Co-pilot   Thanks.

Pilot   We've no idea whether the whole of the nose gear is damaged – I think we _____ [8] to assume it may all collapse when we land.

Co-pilot   Sure – landing with abnormal gear – here it is. First problem is that if the gear collapses then both engine nacelles will contact the runway.

Pilot   _____ [9] we shut down just as we land?

Co-pilot   Yeah – _____ _____ [10] shut down for sure – but I _____ _____ [11] you should leave it too late though. The procedure is to shut down before or during the landing roll. I know you want all the services as long as possible but if I _____ _____ [12], I'd shut down sooner rather than later.

Answer the questions.

1   What does ATC offer to do?
2   What does the co-pilot suggest?
3   What advice or opinion does the pilot give?

INTERACTIONS

6   **Work with a partner to make suggestions or offer help and advice on the next likely course of action.**

PARTNER FILES ➤   Partners A and B   File 14, p. 73

USEFUL LANGUAGE		
Making suggestions	**Offering help**	**Giving advice or opinions**
Couldn't you … ?	Can I help by … ?	If I were you, I'd …
How about … ?	I'll … , shall I?	I (don't) think you should …
I suggest …	Shall I … ?	You'd better …
Let's …	Would you like me to … ?	You ought to …
Perhaps you could …	You should …	
What about … ?		
Why don't you … ?		

COMPREHENSION

AUDIO
48

7   **Listen to the next part of the exchange. Were the air company's suggestions included in your list?**

AUDIO
49

8 **SAS 105 has informed Approach that they are ready to land. Listen. Answer the questions.**

1 What does Approach ask about?
2 What does Approach tell SAS 105 to expect?
3 How many people are on board SAS 105?
4 How long is the foam carpet?

9 **Read part of the newspaper article. Answer the questions.**

PILOT AVERTS TRAGEDY

An A320 belonging to SAS and carrying a total of 237 passengers and 8 crew yesterday made a controlled emergency landing on a foam-covered runway. The pilot skilfully landed the plane, which had jammed landing gear, at reduced speed onto the foam and although it skidded to a halt just beyond the end of the runway, no one was injured. All the rescue services were on standby. The passengers were evacuated unhurt in less than three minutes.

1 Do you know any similar stories of successful emergency landings? What happened?
2 Describe the emergency provisions at your local airport.

10 **Read the first part of the pilot's story. Then answer the questions.**

TEN FEET TOO HIGH

The weather was good – a light wind, great visibility, and almost no cloud. I was five miles out and all set to land. I know the airfield well and joined in the left-hand circuit as usual, number three to land. I could see the other two – one on final and the other one joining from the north, ahead of me. I was at two thousand. I got down to twelve hundred and turned onto downwind, got the gear down, and cut the speed back to about a hundred knots. I was pretty close to number two, so I went out a bit further than usual on the downwind leg, for separation.

Two miles out, I turned onto base. I still had visual with the other two. At a thousand feet, I reduced the thrust and turned onto final. The low sun at that time of day made it a bit difficult to see the runway. I was down to about 85 knots when I heard number two say he was going around. I guess he had problems with the sun in his eyes. I saw number one touch down, and then I heard this horrific bang.

1 What was the weather like?
2 How many aircraft were coming in to land?
3 Why did the pilot extend the downwind leg?
4 What time of day was it?
5 Why did he think the second aircraft decided to go around?

11 **Read the second part of the pilot's story. Then answer the questions.**

The plane shuddered, but everything seemed to be working. I was pretty scared and just wanted to land, which I did without any problems. While I was still on the taxiway, ATC told me to stop and shut down. No one was sure what had happened, but we could see Fire and Rescue coming, so we got right out of the plane. Outside, of course, we could see the damage.

The whole of the upper fin on the tail was ripped apart. I guessed straightaway what had happened. I'd clipped the wires on the pylons. Someone had seen it happen – we'd gone between the two wires hanging from the electricity pylons.

The top of the fin had hit the top wire between the pylons – if I'd been about ten feet lower, I'd have missed them!

1   The diagram below shows his plane (3) over the water, about to join the circuit. Mark the route that the pilot took.
2   Mark any possible alternative route.
3   What other options did the pilot have?

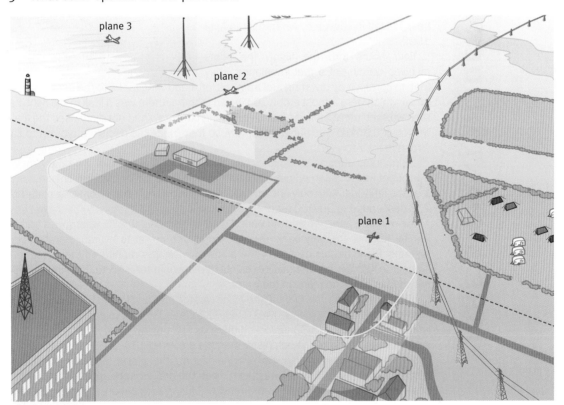

VOCABULARY

12 **Check you understand the meaning of the following landing problems and hazards. Have you experienced any? Which do you think are the most common?**

1   lighting systems failure
2   speed control problems
3   medical emergency
4   diversion
5   tail strike
6   runway incursions and excursions
7   technical problems (e.g., engine failure)
8   braking problems
9   bad surface conditions
10 bad weather
11 delays
12 flock of birds on the runway

AUDIO
⊙
50

Listen to five landing exchanges. For each exchange, write the problem or hazard.

1 _____

2 _____

3 _____

4 _____

5 _____

What is different about the final incident?

OUTPUT

Read the article and answer the questions.

PICHÉ'S GIANT GLIDER

Flight TS 236 left Toronto at 8.52 p.m. on 23 August 2001 with 293 passengers and 13 crew members onboard. The 362-seat Airbus A330 carried 47.9 tonnes of fuel – 5.5 tonnes more than required by regulations. The plane, manufactured in 1999, had been placed in service by Air Transat in April 1999.

Four hours into the flight, the pilots received warning of a fuel imbalance. They tried to correct it by diverting fuel from the left-hand wing tanks to the right-hand wing tanks, which were almost empty. Unknown to them, there was a leak in the right-hand tank, so even more fuel was lost. Even though the crew had not diagnosed the leak, it was clear that fuel was dangerously low, so they made the decision to divert to Lajes Airport in the Azores.

28 minutes after an emergency was declared, engine number 2 on the right wing was out of fuel and flamed out. Captain Piché ordered full thrust from engine number 1 on the left wing. With only one engine, the plane couldn't stay at cruising altitude. TS 236 descended to 30 000 feet.

13 minutes later, engine number 1 flamed out. Flight 236 was now a glider. A ram air turbine, the only back up, supplied limited power to hydraulic and electrical systems. Piché did his best to fly the plane and Dejager monitored the descent rate – about 2000 feet per minute. He calculated it would take 15 to 20 minutes before they had to ditch the plane in the water.

When the air base was in sight, the plane was too high and too fast, so Piché executed a series of side-slipping manoeuvres to lose altitude and slow the plane. They successfully lined up with runway 15/33, unlocked the slats and deployed the landing gear, but the airspeed was 200 knots, much faster than the preferred 130–140 knots.

20 minutes after the second engine failure, the plane landed at about 370 kilometres per hour. Several tyres burst when the brakes were applied, but the plane finally stopped in the middle of the runway. During evacuation, 16 passengers and 2 crew members were injured. 2 passengers suffered serious, but not life-threatening, injuries. Most of the injuries were minor or very minor.

In 2002, Captain Piché was given the Quebec National Assembly's Medal of Honour for his heroic flight and landing of the giant glider that was TS 236.

OVER TO YOU

Do you know any other stories of a pilot using great skill to land a plane safely?

What was the situation?

Do you know any other stories of 'lucky escapes'?

8 On the ground

Look at the diagram. Match the list of names to the numbers on the diagram.

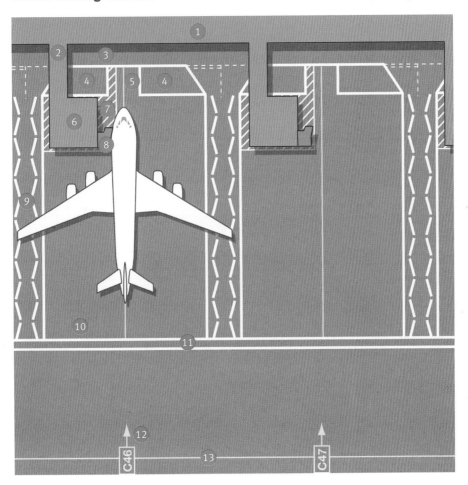

a   airside road
b   stand number and centre line
c   gate room
d   tug area
e   jetty/jetway
f   no parking area
g   interstand clearway

h   low bridge
i   pier
j   stand
k   boundary between apron and taxiway
l   taxilane centreline
m   equipment parking area

What incidents might occur between landing and arrival at the stand?

1   **Look at the pictures of situations on the ground. Match each picture to the correct word or phrase.**

1   congestion

2   giving way

3   a major incident

4   no stand available

5   police/customs inspection

6   a truck going the wrong way

7   a technical problem

8   work in progress

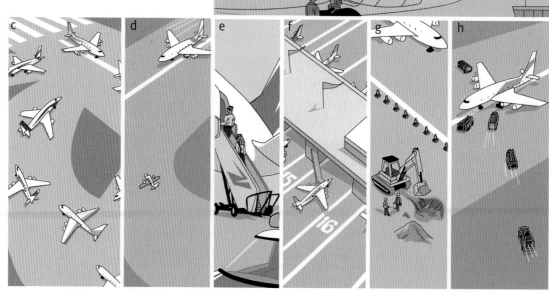

2   **Now match each of the comments with a picture above.**

1   *Can you believe this traffic today! It's like the streets of Bangkok!*

2   *Man, we got red lights all over the place out here.*

3   *It's always this way. I can never find a parking space!*

4   *I'm just letting the big guy get out of the way.*

5   *Whoa! Looks like we got an incursion coming up! Who does he think he is?!*

6   *Looks like that guy's gonna need to see a mechanic before he goes anywhere.*

7   *Hey, you know you got some guys digging a hole out here?*

8   *Looks like he's got some interesting passengers on board – wonder where he's come from.*

Can you paraphrase the above statements using more standard English?

The airport is congested today.

3 Read this incident report. Then answer the questions.

An aircraft with 2 crew and 48 passengers landed on runway 24R and vacated the runway onto the rapid exit taxiway KC, which is 46 metres wide. The weather conditions were clear; it was 50 minutes before sunrise and thus it was dark.

The captain brought the aircraft to a stop at the first junction along the rapid exit taxiway, the intersection with taxiway K and awaited taxi instructions. The tower said, *Proceed via taxiway C hold at C1.*

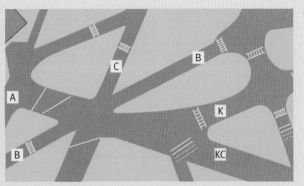

Plan of taxiway intersection KC, C, B

The captain taxied ahead and at the next junction, where he was expecting to turn right onto C, he saw a signboard to his right indicating taxiway A ahead. There are five paved surfaces which intersect at this junction; they are, in anticlockwise direction from the runway exit: KC, B (23m wide), C (23m wide) KC and B (see plan below).

The captain knew the airport and knew taxiway A was beyond taxiway C. Confused by the signboard and thinking that he had somehow passed taxiway C, he advised his co-pilot that he had missed the taxiway and turned hard right to get back to where he thought it was. While he was turning, ATC issued further taxi instructions which the co-pilot needed to write down, taking his attention away from monitoring the aircraft's position. The captain in turning sharply thought he had cleared the edge of the paved area with the nose gear by about 2 metres and believing the aircraft was safely round, he reduced the turning angle.

ATC now advised that he had taken a wrong turn onto taxiway B, so the captain brought the aircraft to a stop. ATC then instructed the aircraft to proceed but as the captain applied power, he realized that the aircraft was stuck; the left main gear had sunk into the edge of the grass between taxiway B and taxiway C.

1 It was dark. Was this a factor in the incident?

2 Mark on the diagram:

   a *X* for where the aircraft first stopped;

   b an arrow showing the route from this point to the intersection;

   c *A* for the likely position of the sign board;

   d an arrow showing the route from the intersection onto the incorrect taxiway;

   e *O* for the position of the left main gear when the pilot finally stopped.

3 Suggest an alternative position for this sign:

4 What do you think were the main recommendations of the incident report?

4 There are three ways to say *–ed* as a past tense ending. The words in the box all come from the report on page 63. Put each word in the correct column.

> reduced • landed • taxied • vacated • turned • missed
> • confused • awaited • realized • instructed

/ɪd/ wanted	/t/ walked	/d/ called

AUDIO

51

Listen and check your answers.

STRUCTURE

5 Now use the pictures to re-tell the story. For each picture, use a word from the box.

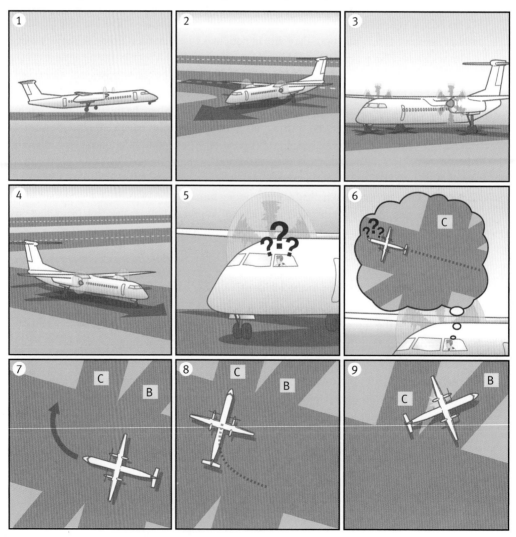

6 **What do you think will happen next? How will the passengers get to the gate? What problems might they have?**

> **SAYING WHAT WILL HAPPEN**
>
> First, the pilot will tell Ground that he needs assistance.
> Then, a truck will come out and help to move the plane.
> They'll need to be careful ... .
> They might have a problem with ... .
> After that, ...
> Finally ... .

INTERACTIONS

7 **Work with a partner to practise saying what will happen.**

PARTNER FILES ▶ Partners A and B File 6, p. 71

COMPREHENSION

AUDIO
52

8 **Listen. First note the call signs of the aircraft or other vehicle. Then listen again and note their location and any other information mentioned.**

	Call sign	Location and other information
1	_____	_____
2	_____	_____
3	_____	_____
4	_____	_____
5	_____	_____
6	_____	_____
7	_____	_____

Answer the questions.

1 How many aircraft are communicating with ATC?
2 What other vehicle requests permission to taxi?

FLUENCY

9 **Clear communication is the key to safety – even getting to the gate. Do you agree or disagree with these six recommendations for clear RT communication?**

		Agree	Disagree
1	Speak slowly.	❑	❑
2	Find different ways of explaining the same thing.	❑	❑
3	Always have a dictionary close to you.	❑	❑
4	Don't worry about grammatical errors.	❑	❑
5	If you don't understand, say so.	❑	❑
6	Use only standard ICAO phraseology.	❑	❑

Discuss your answers with a partner. Say why you agree or disagree.

PRONUNCIATION

10 English uses a lot of words with groups of consonants that sometimes form difficult sounds. Underline them in these words that you heard in exercise 8.

a<u>ckn</u>owle<u>dg</u>e	con<u>str</u>u<u>ct</u>ion
past	continue
front	foxtrot
works	number
ramp	standby

AUDIO

53

Listen and repeat.

FLUENCY

11 Read the article. Then change one word in each sentence below to make them true.

SHUT DOWN, TURN AROUND

The end of a flight often isn't the end of the working day for an airplane. Many planes make four or five trips a day, with an hour on the ground between flights. During this hour, the passengers disembark, their luggage is unloaded, the aircraft is cleaned, refuelled, supplied with in-flight meals, and then reloaded.

What happens if you reduce a one-hour turnaround to 40 minutes? The plane may be able to make six or seven flights in a day. That, of course, means more income for the airline.

Does this mean forcing ground staff to work more quickly? Not necessarily. Research shows that the most time can be gained or lost in the reboarding process. It might seem obvious that loading a plane from back to front would be the quickest way. However, a study by Boeing found that loading from window to aisle significantly reduced boarding time and made turnaround quicker. Now many airlines have adopted this practice, and turnaround times are on the decrease.

Reduced turnaround times can cause problems, however. Small delays early in the day can make a whole series of flights run late. And of course quicker turnaround means more traffic and therefore busier airports.

1 Few planes make more than one trip per day.
2 Airlines can decrease their income by having more flights.
3 Refuelling takes the most time of any turnaround task.
4 Loading the aisle seats first is the quickest.
5 A delay late in the day can cause problems all day long.

OUTPUT Look at the pictures and read the opinions. Then answer the questions.

The future of flight?

The 'supers' are the most fuel-efficient airliners yet. Both have a range of over 8,000 miles, a service ceiling of 43,000 feet, and exceptional noise reduction. These planes will change jet travel forever.

The big airports are just getting bigger – more crowded, harder to move through. The future is in VLJs – very light jets – that can quickly fly into and out of smaller regional airports. One day soon, flying will be like taking a taxi.

Sooner or later, people will have to stop flying so much. There won't be a technological solution. We need to change the way we live.

International travel has greatly improved the life of my family. People from other countries want to visit my country. They bring money and we are happy to host them. It would be terrible if tourism declined.

I can't wait to travel in space. It costs a million dollars now, but in 20 years, who knows? It will be great when ordinary people can take a holiday on the moon.

Do you know oil is going to run out? I think that's good, because then people won't be able to pollute the Earth's atmosphere. Planes are the worst.

OVER TO YOU

Which opinions do you agree with? Which do you disagree with?

How does aviation affect your life? For example, do you buy goods that arrive in your country by air?

Does your country export goods by air?

How would you describe the future of aviation?

Test yourself!

See how much aviation vocabulary you know.
Use the clues to complete the crossword puzzle.

Across

1   A word that means you agree to do something.
5   Someone ... aggressively may be unwell.
6   GHIST: Can you tell me when you've got the field in ... ?
7   CIIINTVY: Avoid the ... until the air display has finished.
8   A unit of atmospheric pressure.
9   A first-aid kit may be useful for minor ... incidents.
11 A fire ... is always carried in the cockpit.
13 CEERSU: An air-sea ... helicopter will assist anyone in trouble at sea.
14 De-... is done pre-flight in winter in cold climates.
15 A unit of speed.
19 Can you ... your heading, please ?
20 Another word for *wait*.
21 A mixture of rain and snow on the runway.
22 A ... on the head may cause a headache.
23 Someone under the influence of alcohol is ... .
25 ILS will lead to the ... path.
26 A pilot may dump ... rather than land heavy.
27 A tyre ... may damage the aircraft.

Down

2   A 360 degree turn.
3   BIIIILSTVY: Blowing snow reduces ... significantly.
4   CEEHILSV: Service ... help with aircraft preparation.
10 EECPTX: What time do you ... to be ready?
12 You'll probably find one at works in progress.
16 On approach, the captain tells the crew *Ten minutes to* ... .
17 Another word for *hold-up*: There's a ... . Your new time slot is at 1500.
18 If I did not understand I ... say S*ay again*.
19 Just before push-back, the ... are removed from the plane's wheels.
20 Mayday is a call for immediate ... .
21 Another word for *gate*.
22 A ...-flop is a gear-up landing.
24 A word that means you have received and understood a message.
28 Name the airside vehicle used for push-back.

Partner Files

UNIT 1, Exercise 3 **File 1**

Partner A

1 Call an Air Traffic Service Unit (ATSU) and pass your message. Use the ICAO phonetic alphabet to spell unfamiliar names.

Communication 1
Gatwick Approach, Speedbird 209. Flight level 110. Heading 100. ETA Isle of Man 1005.

Communication 2
Shanwick Control, BD-744A requesting Oceanic clearance. Estimating 58 West, 10 North at 1310 UTC. Requesting Flight Level 350, Mach .80.

Communication 3
Speedbird 567-A is cleared 16 000 on 1010 hPa. Expect to cross GOOSE level at 120, speed 250 knots.

2 Listen to the communication from Partner B. Record the information you hear.

UNIT 2, Exercise 12 **File 2**

Partner A
Parallel routes across the Atlantic are always busy. Today is especially busy. You are the pilot of a Boeing 767 preparing for a transatlantic flight.
• You are due to push back at 25.
• It is now 1420. Your passengers are still boarding.
• There is also a 10-minute catering delay.
Negotiate a new slot time. You want a slot time of 40.

You begin: *Ground, B767. We are due to push back at 25, but ...*

Continue the conversation:
Can we ... ?
The passengers are ...
We have a problem with ...
We're going to call the catering company and ...
We're going to be ready in ...

UNIT 3, Exercise 12 **File 3**

Partner A
You are ATC Ground. Begin an exchange with Speedbird 556.
Direct Speedbird 556 from stand D12 to the holding point.
Give hazards warnings.
Note additional hazards reported by Speedbird 556.
Begin: *Speedbird 556, push-back approved ...*

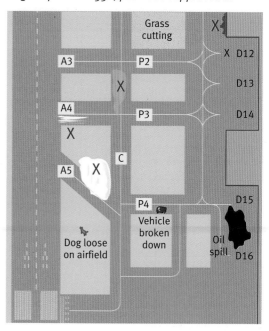

UNIT 4, Exercise 11 **File 4**

Partner A
Give the following information to your partner:

Situation 1
YB, fast moving traffic at 2 o'clock, 6 miles crossing right to left. 1000 feet below.

Situation 2
YB, turn left immediately, heading 270, opposite traffic at 12 o'clock.

Situation 3
YB, stop climb at FL 190 due to converging traffic 10 o'clock, 15 miles, 1,000 feet above.

UNIT 5, Exercise 6   File 5

Partner A

B) 08/02/14 00:01 UTC   C) 08/05/14 23:59
TO HELP WITH FLT PLN, ACFT INBD TO ADVISE
ASAP ON APCH IF UNABLE TO COMPLY WITH SPEED
RESTRICTION.
BE AWARE CRANE OPR AT 138FT AMSL 470M-620M
W OF 09L THR. 180M-290M S OF 09L CL. CRANE TO
BE LOWERED FOR LDG AND DEP ACFT.
BE AWARE TWY A AND TWY M UNAVBL AS PERM
CLSD FM RWY TO TWY Z DUE WIP

Unit 8, Exercise 7   File 6

Partner A and Partner B

Read the report below. With a partner, re-tell the
incident.
First, the pilot vacated ...
Then, he was cleared ...
After that, he reached ... and turned ...
Finally, the wing ...

> **REPORT**
> After landing the pilot vacated the runway to
> the left. He was given clearance to the stand
> via taxiways A and B. When he was abeam
> the threshold he turned left towards the stand
> area. As he turned, his right wing struck the
> edge of a marker board which indicated the
> holding position for the runway.

Now use your own ideas to say what will happen
next.
- Decide whether the incident is likely to be
  hazardous.
- Decide what precautions may be taken.
- Decide what services may be needed.

First, ...
Then, ...
After that, ...
Finally, ...

UNIT 6, Exercise 17   File 7

Partner A

Put the requests in the correct order.
a   you for change Would this tyre me?
b   you truck? move Can this
c   you Do lowering the mind stairs?

Match each request
above to a situation.
Then make each
request to Partner B
and listen to the
response.

Situation 1

Situation 2   Situation 3

Put the responses in the correct order.
a   A320. it's the for Sorry, booked
b   course. Of and Milk sugar?
c   I a back. Sorry, have bad

Listen to Partner B's
request for each situation.
Choose and give the best
response.

Situation 4

Situation 5    Situation 6

UNIT 1, Exercise 3   File 8

Partner B

1 Listen to the communication from Partner A. Record the information you hear.
2 Call an Air Traffic Service Unit (ATSU) and pass your message. Use the ICAO phonetic alphabet to spell unfamiliar names.

Communication 4

London Control, United Air 955. Flight level 90. Heading 230. ETA Saint Abbs Head 1005.

Communication 5

Roger, Prestwick. 317A is cleared 58 North 10 West, 60 North 20 West, 60 North 30 West, 60 North 40 West, 58 North 50 West, PORGY. Maintain 350, Mach .80.

Communication 6

UK Air 298-A Heavy, taxi to hold R for runway 31. QNH 1016. FALCON 4F departure. Squawk 7412.

UNIT 2, Exercise 12   File 9

Partner B

You are a ground controller giving clearance to a transatlantic pilot. On southern routes, a mid-Atlantic depression is causing strong winds and more bad weather is forecast.

- Some flights have already changed to northern routes and these are becoming congested.
- Delays are building up.
- It is now 1420. You can only allow a 12-minute delay.

Listen to B767 and respond:
Yes, you can./No you can't.
I can allow ...
You can delay until ...
There's a problem with ...
Are your passengers ...?
I'm (not) going to allow ...

UNIT 4, Exercise 11   File 10

Partner B

Give the following information to your partner:

Situation 4

YB, look out for slow moving traffic 6 miles ahead of you.

Situation 5

YB, traffic to your right. 6 miles overtaking – heavy – same level.

Situation 6

YB, traffic 9 o'clock, 8 miles parallel. DC 10 1000 feet below, climbing.

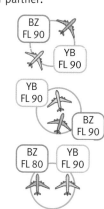

UNIT 3, Exercise 12   File 11

Partner B

You are Speedbird 556 pushing back at D12.
Listen and mark route from stand D12 to the holding point.
Note hazards given by ATC.
Advise ATC of any hazards not given/provided by ATC.
Partner A will begin the exchange.

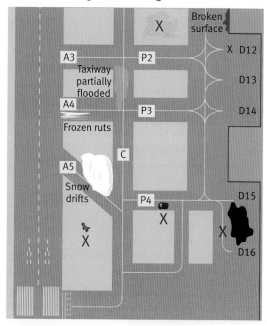

UNIT 5 Exercise 6   File 12

Partner B

B) 08/01/28 09:58 UTC   C) 08/04/28 09:00
NO TWY CL AT INT OF TXY ALPHA AND KILO. ALSO TWY A LGT PARTIALLY U/S AND ONLY AVBL BTN HOLDING POINT ALPHA AND S END OF APRON.
TKOF OBST: TREES MAX HGT 34-57 FT AGL 64-81FT AMSL
BE AWARE CIRCUIT PROC CHANGED. FOLLOWING TKOF RWY 27 HDG IS NOW 210 DEG.
FURTHER INFO AVBL FM TWR 01987 510006

UNIT 6, Exercise 17   File 13

Partner B

Put the responses in the correct order.
a   I the have key. Sorry, don't
b   they're afraid I'm broken.
c   no Sure, problem. take It'll hour. an

Listen to Partner A's request for each situation. Choose and give the best response.

Situation 1

Situation 2   Situation 3

Put the requests in the correct order.
a   for I you coffee? a ask Could
b   gate 51? Would mind if you we at park
c   Would this? you me help with

Match each request above to a situation. Then make each request to Partner A and listen to the response.

Situation 4

Situation 5   Situation 6

UNIT 7, Exercise 6   File 14

Use the procedure for landing with abnormal gear, together with your own knowledge, to do the role play.

Partner A

You are the pilot. Suggest actions to be completed before the landing.
Example: *You'd better prepare the cabin crew for a rough landing.*

Partner B

You are the co-pilot. Give your opinions and advice in response to the pilot's suggestions.
Example: *I'll tell them to get the passengers in brace position for landing, shall I?*

LDG WITH ABNORMAL L/G

PREPARATION
- CABIN CREW .... NOTIFY
- ATC .... NOTIFY
- GALLEY .... OFF
- **IF NOSE L/G abnormal**
  - CG location (if possible) .... AFT

- OXYGEN CREW SUPPLY............................... OFF
- SEAT BELTS/NO SMOKING .... ON
- CABIN and COCKPIT............................. PREPARE

APPROACH
- GPWS SYS.. OFF
- L/G LEVER .... CHECK DOWN
- GRVTY GEAR EXTN
  handcrank................... TURN BACK TO NORMAL
- AUTOBRAKE................................. DO NOT ARM
- EMER EXIT LT .... ON
- CABIN REPORT..................................... OBTAIN

BEFORE LANDING
- BRACE FOR IMPACT .... ORDER

FLARE, TOUCHDOWN AND ROLL OUT
- REVERSE .... DO NOT USE
- • IF NOSE L/G abnormal
  - NOSE .... MAINTAIN UP
  - ENG MASTERS .... OFF

WHEN A/C STOPPED
- ENG and APU FIRE push button .... PUSH
- ENG and APU AGENT .... DISCH
- EVACUATION.. INITIATE

Answer key

UNIT 1

page 5

STARTER

PILOT FLIGHT 71	←→TOWER CONTROLLER
	←→CO-PILOT FLIGHT 71
	←→CABIN CREW FLIGHT 71
	←→PASSENGERS FLIGHT 71
CO-PILOT FLIGHT 71	←→TOWER CONTROLLER
CABIN CREW FLIGHT 71	←→PASSENGERS FLIGHT 71
PILOT G-SC27	←→TOWER CONTROLLER

1

1 a C61 b C63 c C and 3
2 a FL100 b 3800 c *left* and *right*

Possible answers:
Pronunciation – *C63* instead of *Charlie 63*
Structure – *Number give me.*
Vocabulary – confusion of *left* and *right*
Fluency – ATC in exchange 2
Comprehension – Ground in exchange 1
Interactions – both exchanges

page 7

4

1 Are you a controller or a pilot?
2 Do you speak any other languages?
3 Have you ever been abroad?
4 When did you last travel by plane?
5 Does your company provide English training courses?
6 Has your English improved in the last ten minutes?

5
1 b   2 d   3 a   4 e   5 c   6 f

page 8

6
a 2   b 4   c 1   d 5   e 3

7
1 The controller does not understand plain English.
2 Spoke clearly; re-phrased and used different words.
3 Asked a colleague for help.

8

1	violent	5	aggressive
2	unruly	6	ground
3	hit	7	services
4	drunk	8	remove

page 9

9
1 violent, unruly, drunk
2 hit
3 ground

10

1	Occasionally	8	rarely
2	standard	9	sometimes
3	usually	10	often
4	plain	11	local
5	non-standard	12	never
6	unnecessary	13	always
7	usually		

page 10

11

1	keep up	5	check out
2	get back	6	pass over
3	stays up	7	get to
4	come in		

12
1 try
2 Have you got the field in sight?
3 make a low pass
4 a bit longer
5 for the time being
6 let me know
7 check out
8 Can I ...
9 Do you want to ... ?
10 Identified.

13
Exchange 1
Good morning.
Can I keep up this high speed a bit longer?
For the time being, yes. I'll get back to you in a minute.

1 *Good morning* not necessary.
2 Controller allows pilot to continue at high speed.
3 Standard phraseology is preferable here:
   Request maintain 350 knots until way point.
   Affirmative.
   Expect further instructions in one minute.

Exchange 2
will you let me know what your intentions are for the main landing gear?
We'll try to lower the gear again, but if I'm still unable to release the nose gear – if it still stays up, then we'll land with all three up.

Do you want to come in for a low pass? We can
check out your landing gear when you pass over.
Have you got the field in sight?
When I get to you the gear should be down.
OK, make a low pass over runway two tree for a
landing gear check.

1 Nose gear.
2 Visual check of landing gear – low pass over
  runway 23.
3 Land with all three sets of gear up.

page 11

14
Possible answers:
Situation 1: Can you confirm any reports of wind
shear?
Situation 2: Say again reason for priority landing.
Situation 3: Tower, light aircraft crossing. Can you
please confirm clear to land?
Situation 4: B757, Tower. (This would be repeated
until a response was received.)

UNIT 2

page 13

STARTER
1 Beriev Be-103 amphibious plane
2 Airbus A300-600ST Super Transporter Cargo
  Aircraft
3 Cessna Skycatcher light aircraft
4 Gulfstream executive jet
5 Airbus A380 airliner
6 Sikorsky S61N helicopter

1

A		B		C	
1	b	1	c	1	c
2	a	2	b	2	b
3	c	3	a	3	a

page 14

2

1	h	10	p
2	d	11	m
3	r	12	i
4	e	13	l
5	f	14	j
6	g	15	k
7	c	16	o
8	b	17	q
9	a	18	n

3

1	checks	9	wear
2	surfaces	10	leading
3	strike	11	engine
4	lightning	12	blades
5	foreign	13	fuselage
6	vehicles	14	doors
7	damage	15	hatches
8	undercarriage		

page 15

4
Possible answers:
A flight manuals
B smoke hood, medical kit, oxygen bottle
C pilot (searching cockpit)
D aircraft documents
E load sheet
F pilot, checklist

5

1	b	D		4	a	B
2	c	E		5	d	F
3	e	A		6	f	C

6
Items to carry:
registration certificate, air operator certificate,
insurance certificate, environmental (noise)
limitation certificate, aircraft radio licence, NOTOC =
NOtice TO Captain (= dangerous goods notification
to captain), air worthiness certificate, instruction
manuals, oxygen bottles, first aid kit, and other
equipment

Items not to carry:
suspicious items/explosives

7
1 troubleshooting
2 medical kit
3 dangerous substances
4 routine procedures
5 stowed
6 smuggled

picture A:
Reference books, such as manuals and handbooks,
can be used to check non-routine procedures if
anything unusual occurs during the flight.

picture B:
The portable oxygen cylinder can be used in a
medical emergency or for high-altitude flying in a
small plane; the smoke hood can be used if there
are fumes or smoke in the cockpit; the medical kit is
used for medical emergencies.

picture C:
Security screening of baggage, airline staff, and
passengers; personal searches; restrictions on
amounts and content of baggage.

picture D:
Aircraft registration certificate, air operator's certificate, insurance certificate, environmental (noise) limitation certificate, radio operator authorization

picture E:
NOTOC informs the captain of any materials on board that may require special handing or procedures in the event of an emergency, e.g. chemicals which may support combustion/produce toxic fumes, radioactive materials, live animals, etc.

picture F:
Possible problems:
difficulty securing doors and/or hatches, damage to fuselage/door seals during loading, cracked windscreen, problems with the radio, damage to engine/fan blades following bird ingestion, hydraulic fluid/oil/water/toilet leaks, mismatch between actual load and documentation, lack of wheelchair provision for disabled passenger, low tyre pressure, damaged tyre, faulty lights, obstructed pitot tube

page 16

8
1 The first one uses standard phraseology. The second uses plain English.
2 No standard phraseology for non-routine event.

9
Exchange 1
1 b   2 a
Exchange 2
1 a   2 c   3 b
Exchange 3
1 c   2 a   3 d   4 b

1 A radio problem. (He's not transmitting well.)
2 He thought he needed documents to take a live snake into Malaysia.
3 Yes. The computer failed and didn't produce a strip.

page 17

10
● ▪ cargo, problem, something, pitot
▪ ● control, unload, delay

11
Possible answers:
1 Cargo loaders say we have a problem with the cargo door.
2 There's something wrong with the baggage loader.
3 There's a problem with the stairs.
4 Your cargo door is open.
5 There's oil on the apron.
6 I can see a chock blocking your way.

page 18

13
1 airport name
2 ATIS phonetic alphabet code (e.g. information Bravo)
3 Zulu time
4 instrument approach procedures in use
5 wind direction and speed
6 visibility
7 cloud cover/ceiling
8 temperature
9 dewpoint
10 altimeter setting
11 runway(s) in use
12 relevant NOTAMs or weather advice/remarks or other information

14
1 c		3 d		5 a		7 c
2 b		4 b		6 d		8 c

15
1 Luton
2 Bravo
3 1355
4 300 degrees at 8 knots
5 5 km
6 3000 overcast
7 15
8 8
9 QNH 998 hPa
10 approach 26 left and 26 right. Departures 26 right
11 none

page 19

16
1 j		6 h	
2 b		7 d	
3 c		8 e	
4 f		9 a	
5 g		10 i	

17
message 1: picture 1
message 2: picture 4
message 3: picture 3
message 4: picture 2
message 5: picture 10

UNIT 3

page 21

STARTER
1 c	G		7 h	G	
2 d	G		8 i	SG	
3 b	G		9 g	SN	
4 e	SN		10 j	SG	
5 f	SN		11 a	G	
6 l	SG		12 k	SN	

page 22

1

1	h	spraying icy wings
2	j	transporting passengers
3	e	putting out fires
4	a	carrying cargo
5	c	delivering kerosene
6	i	transporting construction materials
7	f	repairing flat tyres
8	g	reversing planes
9	d	getting rid of compacted ice
10	b	clearing debris

page 23

2

1	BA bus number 5	5	UAL 439
2	RYR 372	6	fire tender
3	de-icer	7	RYR 355
4	maintenance truck	8	sweeper

3

1 d   2 c   3 e   4 f   5 a   6 b

4

1	e	3	d	5	f
2	b	4	c	6	a

5

1   2
2   He's got a radio problem.
3   757 on taxiway Z
4   She's got a problem, a flat tyre.
5   Taxi slowly = move forward at a slow speed. Taxi with caution = be very careful moving forward.

page 24

6

1	should	4	are allowed to
2	mustn't	5	have to
3	don't have to		

7

1	down	4	around
2	off	5	on
3	back	6	up

8

1   Can I <u>change</u> <u>stand</u>?
2   I have to be <u>near</u> our <u>maintenance</u> area.
3   I have a <u>flat</u> <u>tyre</u> on the <u>nose</u> <u>gear</u>.
4   <u>Hang</u> <u>on</u> a minute.
5   Did you <u>get</u> my <u>message</u>?

page 25

9

1   Taxi with <u>caution</u> due to <u>works</u>.
2   Hey, I can see <u>lots</u> of <u>works</u>.
3   Request <u>closest</u> available <u>stand</u>.
4   Is that <u>possible</u>?
5   I <u>don't</u> want to be <u>difficult</u>.

10

1	b	3	c	5	f
2	a	4	d	6	e

11

1	on	3	at	5	on
2	at	4	at	6	with

page 26

13

1   Because a snowplough is going towards the intersection
2   Because the de-icing has been done and now she is delayed
3   Yes, she lost one slot time and is concerned that she will lose the new one.
4   40
5   No, she has to wait.
6   To wait for the snowplough and sweeper
7   Gusting winds and wind shear
8   Snow banks and compacted snow

14

A
1   dense fog
2   gusting winds
3   severe thunderstorms

B
4   flash flooding
5   broken clouds
6   blowing dust

C
7   drifting snow
8   scattered showers
9   tropical storms

Possible answers, but students can give more specific answers using places in their own country as examples:
1   dry, desert areas
2   northern latitudes
3   anywhere that receives most of its rain during one season
4   desert areas
5   moderate maritime climates
6   coastal regions; the term is usually for tropical storms in the North Atlantic Ocean
7   moderate maritime climates
8   coastal regions; the term is usually for tropical storms in the Western Pacific

15

1 F	3 F	5 F
2 T	4 T	6 F

16

Technical problems: breakdown, malfunction, mechanical problems, engine failure, engine stall and surge, jammed doors

Human factors: unruly passengers, sick passengers, sick pilot

Weather conditions: de-icing, flash flooding, heavy snowfall, poor visibility

Emergencies: collisions, engine on fire, medical emergency, terrorism

Other causes: fuel spillage, de-icing, being stuck in the mud, police/customs control, blocked runway, runway incursion, industrial action, lost luggage, animal on the runway

page 27

17

Possible answers:

1 There's a burst tyre.
2 The door won't close.
3 Customs seem to be going on to the plane.
4 The engine is on fire.
5 The pilot appears to be sick.
6 There's a horse on the runway.

18

a major engine failure

page 28

20

Sample answer:

Ground: Iberia 324, proceed to holding point Lima and prepare for departure.

Pilot 324: Iberia 324. Proceeding to holding point Lima. Will report when ready for departure.

Ground: Iberia 324, hold at intersection Delta Alpha. We have traffic problems, so expect some delay.

Pilot 324: Roger control, will hold at the intersection and await further instructions. Iberia 324.

Ground: Iberia 324, I'm pleased to say the traffic problems are over, continue to holding point Lima, prepare for departure.

Pilot 324: Iberia 324. Thanks for that, continuing to holding point Lima, prepare for departure.

Ground: Iberia 324, line up and hold.

Pilot 324: Iberia 324. Line up and wait, ready for departure.

Ground: Iberia 324, cleared for take-off.

Pilot 324: Cleared for take-off. Iberia 324.

UNIT 4

page 29

1

a 7	c 4	e 3	g 6
b 1	d 5	f 2	

1 vehicles on the runway; plane entered runway at wrong point
2 BVL
3 6 miles
4 right
5 *Continue heading ...*
6 130 degrees
7 15 knots

Final responses

b (1) We'll need to file a report on this right away.

f (2) Maintaining flight level 190. Left turn heading 270 after GANET. BVL.

e (3) Descending immediately flight level 80, N355.

c (4) Climbing 120 heading 350. Call you reaching GBL.

d (5) Maintaining 6000 feet. Heading 050. N3E.

g (6) Climbing flight level 160. Heading 130. D6V.

a (7) Confirm fire brigade on the way.

page 30

2

1 b	3 g	5 f	7 d
2 a	4 c	6 e	

3

/s/	/ʃ/	/tʃ/
service	wish	change
instead	sure	check
sorry		approach
say		

4

1 Did	4 Did
2 Are	5 rather
3 instead	6 Can

Affirmative: Yeah, it's fine. Yep, that's fine. Yes, please. As you wish. Sure.
Negative: Sorry, no.

page 31

5

1 above	5 near	9 behind
2 on	6 in front of	10 next to
3 at	7 over	11 into
4 across	8 beyond	12 below

6

1 above/next to   2 language

page 32

7

1	across	5	in front of
2	into	6	behind
3	above	7	next to
4	below	8	beyond

8

1	g	3	b	5	h	7	f
2	c	4	d	6	e	8	a

9

1	e	3	f	5	c	7	d
2	b	4	a	6	g	8	h

page 33

10

1 Look out for <u>slow</u>-moving traffic <u>six miles ahead</u>.
2 <u>Avoiding</u> action. Turn <u>left</u> immediately, heading <u>125</u>.
3 <u>Opposite</u> traffic at <u>12</u> o'clock.
4 Traffic to your <u>left</u> <u>two</u> miles. <u>Overtaking</u> FL <u>90</u>.
5 <u>Fast-moving</u> traffic at 2 o'clock crossing <u>right</u> to <u>left</u>.
6 <u>Conflicting</u> traffic at <u>6</u> o'clock.
7 Traffic 5 o'clock <u>parallel</u>. 1000 feet <u>below</u>, <u>climbing</u>.
8 <u>Maintain</u> FL <u>150</u> until further advised.
9 You're <u>well</u> <u>clear</u> of traffic.

11

Students' drawings should match the ones in the corresponding Partner File.

12

1	some	3	any	5	any	7	any
2	some	4	some	6	any	8	some

page 34

13

Possible answers:
Pilot reports –
AMX 341: Severe turbulence after FALCON.
SHD 24: Wind shear on leaving Lahoa.
BMM 38: CB cloud/moderate icing after PUFIN.
AFL 397: Moderate turbulence at WADER.
BEE 26: Moderate turbulence at WADER.

ATC warnings –
CFP 86, hail storm ahead.
AFL 397, slow-moving traffic ahead.
BAW 63, moderate turbulence at WADER.
BEE 26, moderate turbulence, severe icing, CB cloud ahead.
BMM 38, scattered cloud ahead.
SHD 24, severe turbulence after FALCON.
RMV 242, thick fog ahead.

page 35

14

The vibration was caused by tyre debris from the tyre burst entering number one engine.

15

1	Before	4	As soon as
2	When	5	After
3	While	6	Once, until

page 36

16

Possible answers:
1 Loose or broken fan blade, bird ingestion, door not properly locked, nose-wheel shimmy, compressor stall
2 Can cause plane to skid off runway, wheel damage
3 Because of the damage to the engine
4 Students' own answers

UNIT 5

page 37

STARTER

1 hot air balloons
2 fuel dumping
3 weather balloon
4 in-flight refuelling
5 air display
6 demolition of explosives
7 hang gliding
8 parachute jumping

1

1	d	3	a	5	e
2	c	4	b		

Not pictured: inoperable warning light, fireworks display

page 38

2

1 approximately 4 miles north-east of current position drifting right to left
2 inoperable warning light
3 fuel dumping
4 in-flight refuelling
5 30 minutes

3

Air display and associated intense aerial activity including jet and propeller aircraft plus helicopters. No aircraft is to fly within an area of circle radius 3.5 nautical miles, centred at fifty two degrees and five minutes North zero degrees eight minutes East unless approved by Air Traffic Control.
Pilots to exercise caution in the vicinity. For Operations information contact telephone number 07780-870-476.

4

	Activity	1000	1200	1400	1600
Merthyr	hang gliding	no	yes	yes	yes
Land's End	free-fall parachuting	yes	no	no	no
Brecon Beacons	fighters training	no	yes	yes	yes
Bath	hot air balloon event	no	yes	yes	no
Hatfield	laser testing	no	no	no	no

5

/ə/	/ʌ/	/ɪ/
balloon	dumping	display
until	jumping	downwind
avoid		

/e/	/æ/	/eɪ/
testing	parachute	laser
demolition	hang	training
		delay

/əʊ/	/aɪ/
explosives	fighters
zero	flight
controlled	gliding

6

Student A example answer:
This warning is for February the 14th, 2008, from 0001 hours until May the 14th 2359 hours co-ordinated universal time. To help with flight planning, aircraft inbound should advise as soon as possible on approach if they are unable to comply with speed restrictions. Be aware of a crane operating at 138 feet above mean sea level, 470 metres to 620 metres west of runway 09 left threshold and 180 metres to 290 metres south of runway 09 left centreline. The crane will be lowered for landing and departing aircraft. Be aware that taxiway A and taxiway M are unavailable because they're permanently closed from the runway to taxiway Z owing to work in progress.

Student B example answer:
This warning is for January the 28th, 2008, from 0958 hours until 0900 hours co-ordinated universal time on April the 28th, 2008. There is no taxiway centreline at the intersection of taxiways A and K. Also, the taxiway A lighting is partially unserviceable, and only available between holding point A and the south end of the apron. There is a take-off obstacle: trees with a maximum height of 34 to 57 feet above ground level, which is 64 to 81 feet above mean sea level. Be aware that the circuit procedure has changed. Following take off from runway 27, the heading is now 210 degrees. Further information is available from the tower on 01987 510006.

7

1
a better
b more comfortable
c further

2
a slowest
b more serious

3
a nearest
b stronger

8

Students own answers. Possible answers:
The A380 is the newest plane.
The A380 has the longest range.
The biplane is smaller than the A380.
The twin-engine plane is bigger than the biplane.

9

Possible answers:
1 Exchange 2
2 Exchange 1
3 Exchanges 2 and 3
Unlikely to get worse: turbulence, suspected tyre burst, icing, overflight/clearance refusal
May get worse: fumes in cabin, air rage/drunk, animals loose, warning lights, smoke alarms, bird strikes, suspicion of possible structural failure
May become life threatening: Serious fire in cabin
Life threatening now: loss of engine power/unable to maintain height, explosive decompression

10

1 b	3 c	5 a	7 c	9 c
2 b	4 c	6 a	8 b	10 a

12

1
a Yes.
b Six miles.
2
a An engine fell off.
b Runway 6 left.
3
a There may be an oil leak.
b The Fire Service board after the passengers disembark.

13

1 e	3 i	5 h	7 d	9 b
2 g	4 f	6 c	8 a	10 j

14

1 e	3 c	5 i
2 b	4 h	6 d

15

1 Testing Lewis's skills, or possibly joking
2 My instructor has collapsed.
3 Students' own answers

UNIT 6

page 46

1

Part 1

1 Flight 276 has joined the hold at Wessex Airport, where there are severe delays.
2 Jet blast damage just behind the threshold
3 Before 2300
4 Noise abatement regulations
5 At least half an hour

Part 2

1 Quite a while   2 Descends to 6000 feet

Part 3

1 Divert to Exeter
2 Because the noise curfew is going to take effect

2

1	W	3	H	5	H	7	W
2	H	4	W	6	W		

3

1	c	3	a	5	b
2	d	4	e	6	f

page 47

4

Possible answers:

It snowed four days ago. The snowstorm lasted from 1000 to 2400.

They cleared the runway three days ago. It took six hours.

There was heavy fog two days ago. It lasted for two and a half hours.

It was sunny one day ago. The sunshine lasted from 1145 to 1600.

There was a thunderstorm until a few minutes ago. It lasted for four hours.

5

1	apologize	5	apologies
2	afraid	6	know
3	can't land	7	continue
4	diverted	8	available

page 48

6

1 e 2 f 3 a 4 b 5 d 6 c

7

Possible answers:

If you set the QNH on your altimeter, it will read 65' at touchdown.

If you arrive from the east, you'll use approach frequency 129.8.

If you want to know the altimeter setting in hPa, you'll have to request it.

If you miss your approach, you'll climb on 099° to 3040 feet.

If you follow track 099° at 2040 feet, you'll intercept the glideslope.

8

plane a	AFL 339	plane d	AUA 26
plane b	DLH 1390	plane e	BAW 34
plane c	AZA 29	plane f	BAW 440

9

1	2400 metres	5	1008
2	26	6	220 knots
3	28	7	190 knots
4	1500 metres		

Other measurements that can be expressed in a variety of units – speed: ms^{-1} (correctly said as metres to the minus one, but often just said as metres per second); m/s (metres per second); km/h (kilometres per hour); knot; mph (miles per hour); Mach. Pressure: MB (millibar); hPa (hectopascal); atm (atmosphere); mmHg (millimetres of mercury). Temperature: K (Kelvin); °C (degrees Celsius or centigrade); °F (degrees Fahrenheit)

page 50

10

1 Information Romeo
2 time 2000 Z
3 cloud ceiling 8000 scattered
4 visibility 14 km
5 temperature 44 °C
6 wind 310°, 8 kt
7 altimeter 30.00 mmHg
8 expect ILS or visual to runways 24 and 33
9 advise on first contact you have information Romeo

12

The pilot probably got distracted while he was preparing to land.

13

Possible reasons for going around: weather conditions, runway conditions, landing gear problems, concerns about speed and weight, an obstruction on the runway

1 180 knots
2 mix of slush and rain, standing water
3 KLM 405 is heavy and fast for conditions

page 51

14

1 KLM 405 asks about the runway.
2 Approach says it's wet with some aquaplaning and good braking action.

15

1 d   2 c   3 a   4 b

16
1   *Hang on* signifies a change of plan.
2   There's a lot of traffic.
3   heading 060
4   b
5   a

17
Situation 1
A   Can you move this truck?
B   Sorry, I don't have the key.

Situation 2
A   Do you mind lowering the stairs?
B   I'm afraid they're broken.

Situation 3
A   Would you change this tyre for me?
B   Sure, no problem. It'll take an hour.

Situation 4
B   Could I ask you for a coffee?
A   Of course. Milk and sugar?

Situation 5
B   Would you mind if we park at gate 51?
A   Sorry, it's booked for the A320.

Situation 6
B   Would you help me with this?
A   Sorry, I have a bad back.

18
1   2500 feet
2   The QNH setting was wrong.
3   A tall mast in the vicinity
4   An operational problem

UNIT 7

page 54

1

1 e	3 a	5 b	7 c
2 d	4 f	6 g	

page 55

2
1   monsoon downpour
2   belly-flopped
3   retracted
4   followed process to the letter
5   contamination
6   skidded off
7   Extra familiarization

page 56

3

●•	●••	•●•	••●•	•●••
skidding	landing-gear	configured	information	inadequate
hangar	belly-flopped	retracted		
downpour	slippery	reported		
	incident			

5
1   why don't
2   Would
3   like
4   perhaps
5   could
6   I'll
7   shall
8   ought
9   Couldn't
10 you'd better
11 don't think
12 were you

page 57

1   Connect the pilot with the company.
2   Check the handbook.
3   He assumes the gear will collapse on landing. He suggests shutting down on landing.

page 58

8
1   the fuel situation
2   a foam carpet
3   245 (237 passengers and 8 crew)
4   700 metres

10
1   good: light wind, great visibility, almost no cloud
2   3
3   to increase separation from the plane in front
4   evening (sunset)
5   He thought the sun might have been a factor.

page 59

11
1   The line should go from plane 3 to the orange line just behind plane 2. It then follows the yellow circuit line onto the crosswind and downwind legs to above the houses, where it continues straight over the power lines (rather than following the left turn of the yellow line onto the usual base leg). It turns left above the power lines, then left again in line with the yellow final approach line, where plane 1 is currently shown. Finally, it goes between the wires of the power lines and joins the yellow final approach line.
2   Students' own answers
3   Students' own answers

page 60

12
1   heavy slush and braking concerns
2   some lighting missing, some lighting was too bright
3   heavy rain, strong crosswinds, and wind shear
4   vortex wake
5   passenger with a heart attack

The final incident is a pan-pan call, therefore an urgency message.

Unit 8

page 61

STARTER

1	i	5	d	9	g	13	l
2	h	6	c	10	j		
3	a	7	f	11	k		
4	m	8	e	12	b		

Possible answers:
aquaplaning, collision, wrong turn, flat tyre, hitting
an animal, and others

page 62

1

1	c	3	h	5	e	7	b
2	d	4	f	6	a	8	g

2

Possible answers:
1 c The airport is congested today.
2 h The emergency services are out.
3 f My stand is unavailable.
4 d I'm giving way to a larger aircraft.
5 a There's an unauthorized vehicle approaching
      the runway.
6 b That plane appears to have a serious
      mechanical problem.
7 g Maintenance workers are making a hole in
      the ground.
8 e Customs officials are inspecting that aircraft.

page 63

3

1 No, all the signboards were illuminated and the
   weather was clear.

2

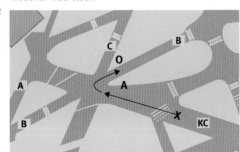

3 Students' own answers
4 Possible answer: trial surface markings in addition
   to signboards and review positions of signboards.

page 64

4

/ɪd/	/t/	/d/
landed	reduced	taxied
vacated	missed	turned
awaited		confused
instructed		realized

5

Possible answers:
The plane landed and vacated the runway. Then the
captain awaited instructions. He was given them,

and taxied ahead. While taxiing, he was confused
by a signboard. He thought he had missed taxiway
C, so he turned hard right and then he reduced the
turning angle. Finally, he realized he was stuck.

page 65

8

1	American 99	holding behind 757; cleared to gate 47
2	Delta 31	short of M; cleared to stand 54; has to give way to A320
3	921 heavy	short of MA; cleared to gate
4	Maintenance 21	stand 27; cleared to L via Z and A
5	Jetblue	reports an incursion by a flat-bed truck
6	China 982	holding; confusion about directions left/right
7	Freedom 6182	blocked by Air China; cleared to gate 52

1 Six aircraft are communicating with ATC.
2 A maintenance vehicle.

page 66

10

ac<u>kn</u>owledge	con<u>st</u>ruction
pa<u>st</u>	con<u>t</u>inue
<u>fr</u>ont	fo<u>xt</u>rot
wor<u>ks</u>	nu<u>mb</u>er
ra<u>mp</u>	stan<u>db</u>y

11

1 ~~Few~~ Many planes make more than one trip per
   day.
2 Airlines can ~~decrease~~ increase their income by
   having more flights.
3 ~~Refueling~~ Reboarding takes the most time of any
   turnaround task.
4 Loading the aisle seats ~~first~~ last is the quickest.
   Loading the ~~aisle~~ window seats first is the
   quickest.
5 A delay ~~late~~ early in the day can cause problems
   all day long.

page 69

1	wilco	17	delay
2	orbit	18	would
3	visibility	19	(across) confirm
4	vehicles		(down) chocks
5	behaving	20	(across) hold
6	sight		(down) help
7	vicinity	21	(across) slush
8	millibar		(down) stand
9	medical	22	(across) bump
10	expect		(down) belly
11	extinguisher	23	drunk
12	tractor	24	roger
13	rescue	25	glide
14	icing	26	fuel
15	knot	27	burst
16	landing	28	tug

Transcripts

Exchange 1

Ground	Er … 363, start up and push at 05.
Pilot 363	Tower, er 363, just started pushing back now. You do know there's another plane pushing back from the next stand?
Ground	Say again 363.
Pilot 363	There's another pushing back on the next stand. We've had to stop.
Ground	Er, 363, stand number give me.
Pilot 363	Er, say again.
Ground	Number give me. Your number, please?
Pilot 363	Er – we're 363.
Ground	No, I ask you stand number.
Pilot 363	Oh, you want our stand number. Yeah – we're on Charlie 61. 363.
Ground	363, you not C63?
Pilot 363	Negative. We're definitely on Charlie 61. 363.
Ground	Ah! Sorry, sir. Stand Charlie 61.

Exchange 2

ATC	X7420, confirm heading 040.
Pilot X7420	Roger, heading 040.
ATC	X7420, turn right, heading 340.
Pilot X7420	Did you hear that? He did say right, didn't he? Er – can you confirm that, please? X7420.
ATC	X7 – er – X – er 420. Right turn heading 3 – er – 40. Climb – er – flight level 1 – er – oo.
Pilot X7420	That's what I thought. Does this guy know right from left? I'm sure that should be left – I'm going to check again. Er – Control – please confirm right onto heading 340. X7420.
ATC	X7420, turn – er – right – er – heading 340.
Pilot X7420	Roger, OK. We're at 3800. If that's what he wants, that's what we'll do.
ATC	X7420, turn left, left. I say again – turn left!

Communication 1

Gatwick Approach, Speedbird 209. Flight level 110. Heading 100. ETA Isle of Man 1005.

Communication 2

Shanwick Control, BD744A requesting Oceanic clearance. Estimating 58 West, 10 North at 1310 UTC. Requesting flight level 350, Mach .80.

Communication 3

Speedbird 567A is cleared 16 000 on 1010 hectopascals. Expect to cross GOOSE – Golf Oscar Oscar Sierra Echo – level at 120, speed 250 knots.

Communication 4

London Control, United Air 955. Flight level 90. Heading 230. ETA Saint Abbs Head 1005.

Communication 5

Roger Prestwick, 317A is cleared 58 North, 10 West, 60 North, 20 West, 60 North, 30 West, 60 North, 40 West, 58 North, 50 West, PORGY– Papa Oscar Romeo Golf Yankee. Maintain 350 Mach .80.

Communication 6

UK Air 298A Heavy. Taxi to hold R for runway 31. QNH 1016. FALCON 4F departure. FALCON – Foxtrot Alpha Lima Charlie Oscar November. Squawk 7412.

Exchange 1

Er – yeah. Good morning there, Quality 405. A departing 747 reported wind shear at 800 feet. Airspeed loss 25 knots, strong right shift. Let me know if you have a problem, please. And – have a nice flight! Bye.

Exchange 2

BAW 456	Speedbird 456 request descent.
Approach	Speedbird 456 maintain flight level 260 expect descent after HERON.
BAW 456	Maintaining flight level 260. Speedbird 456.

Exchange 3

038-NT	Bellevue Tour, 038-NT, nous avons les installations en vue. Pourrait-on envisager une approche à vue main droite pour la 31 droite?
Tower	038-NT, vous me confirmez le terrain en vue?
N97962	Er – Bellevue Tower. Stinson N97962. Request vectors to base-leg 31 right.
Tower	Stinson N97962. Yeah – go ahead …
038-NT	Affirm NT, nous avons les installations en vue.
Tower	Alors autorisé approche à vue main droite 31 droite, NT.
N97962	Er – Bellevue Tower Stinson N97962, I say again. Request vectors to base-leg 31 right.

Exchange 4

A48BX	BX ready for take-off. Request left turn out heading 300 degrees.
Departure	BX, left turn cleared. After departure climb not above altitude 2000 feet until reaching zone boundary.
A48BX	Left turn approved. Climbing to 2000 feet until reaching zone boundary. BX.

Exchange 5

Er – hi, there N526. You've got a south westerly blowing in there. Around about 10 knots. You're OK to land. Runway 28.

UNIT 1, EXERCISE 7

7

Blaze 606	Tukubu Tower, Blaze 606. We have a problem and we'd like a priority landing. We have a violent passenger on board.
Tower 1	Say again 606. I don't understand.
Blaze 606	We have an unruly passenger on board. We have a violent passenger. He has hit a member of the cabin crew. Request priority landing.
Tower 1	606, I'm sorry, sir. I do not understand your problem, sir.
Blaze 606	This passenger is endangering the safety of the flight. He is drunk.
Tower 1	The safety of the flight is in danger?
Blaze 606	Affirm. We have an aggressive passenger. We need to get on the ground as soon as possible.
Tower 2	606, understand you have a problem with a passenger, sir? Do you need medical assistance?
Blaze 606	Negative. We have a medical doctor on board and do not need medical assistance. We need services to remove this unruly passenger from the plane.
Tower 2	606, the police and the airport authorities will meet you, sir.

UNIT 1, EXERCISE 11

8

Exchange 1

Approach	Wolfair 60, good morning. Identified. Proceeding into Alba. Vectoring 05.
Wolfair 60	Direct Alba 05, Wolfair 60. Can I keep up this high speed a bit longer? Wolfair 60.
Approach	Wolfair 60. For the time being, yes. I'll get back to you in a minute.

Exchange 2

Tower	B67, will you let me know what your intentions are for the main landing gear?
B67	Roger. We'll try to lower the gear again, but if I'm still unable to release the nose gear – if it still stays up – then we'll land with all three up. B67.

Tower	B67, do you want to come in for a low pass? We can check out your landing gear when you pass over.
B67	OK, roger. B67.
Tower	B67, have you got the field in sight?
B67	B67, affirm. When I get to you the gear should be down. B67.
Tower	B67, roger. OK, make a low pass over runway 23 for a landing gear check.

UNIT 2, EXERCISE 8

9

Exchange 1

BR 553	Luton Tower, Big Red 553. Radio check 121.2.
Tower	Big Red 553, Luton Tower. Readability 5.
BR 553	Big Red 553.

Exchange 2

Tower	963, it looks as though your pitot head cover is still on. Would you please check?

UNIT 2, EXERCISE 9

10

Exchange 1

BAW 305	Ground, Speedbird 305. Radio check box 1 on 119.4.
Ground	Say again, calling.
BAW 305	Speedbird 305. I want to do a radio check on box 1. 119.4, please.
Ground	Sorry – you're totally unreadable.

Exchange 2

FDX 36	Er, yes. Ground, I want to check on the load today. Fedex 36.
Ground	Fedex 36, go ahead, sir.
FDX 36	I've got a quantity of aerosols – for insect spraying. They're OK, but I've got a live snake on board, and there's no documentation. Fedex 36.
Ground	Fedex 36, no sir. There's no special documentation needed.
FDX 36	You're sure? Won't I need documents on arrival in Kuala Lumpur? Fedex 36.
Ground	Fedex 36 no, it's fine sir. You don't need any documents for Malaysia now.

Exchange 3

B344	Ground, request start-up. B344.
Ground	Sorry, B344. I've no flight plan for B344. Stand by. I'll check you out.
B344	Ground, the plan was filed a couple of hours ago. B344.
Ground	B344, my apologies. The computer has failed again and so that's obviously the reason.
B344	While we're waiting for our clearance, is there a clear area we can taxi to? I want to do a run-up. B344.
Ground	B344, stand by. I'll get back to you very shortly.

OK, er, B344 – I have your flight plan. Start-up approved. The temperature is plus 17.

12 Gatwick Information Hotel, 1755 automated weather. Wind 260 degrees, 15 knots, gusting 27 knots, visibility 6 kilometres, light snow, broken 2600, overcast 3500. Temperature -5, dew point -11, QNH 997 hectopascals. ILS runway 23 left approach in use. Landing runway 23 left, departing runway 23 right. Notice to airmen runway 18 closed. Read back all runway assignments and hold short instructions. Use caution for birds in the vicinity of the active runway. Advise the controller on initial contact you have Hotel.

13 Luton International information Bravo, weather at 1355 UTC. Wind 300 at 8 knots, visibility 5 kilometres. Few 1200, scattered 3000, overcast 5000, temperature 15, dew point 8. QNH 998 hectopascals. IFR approach is ILS or visual, runway 26 left and runway 26 right. Departures, runway 26 right. GPS approaches available. VFR aircraft say direction of flight. All aircraft read back all hold short instructions. Inform ATC that you have information Bravo.

Message 1

14 Lahoa FIR SIGMET timed 1200 hours. Volcanic cloud reported drifting south west of Lahoa from 2000 up to 10 000 feet.

Message 2

Tripoli VOLMET special broadcast at 0030. Heavy sandstorm reported south of Tripoli from ground level up to 9000 feet. Tripoli airport closed. Special SIGMET.

Message 3

Antalya VOLMET special broadcast at 1000. Antalya airport closed due to earth tremors.

Message 4

X-1234, heavy storms approaching the vicinity of the airport. Also, severe wind shear reported at 800 feet during last 30 minutes. Suggest you delay your departure.

Message 5

Strong wind warning. Initially gusts around 25 knots but gradually increasing during the afternoon to reach 35 knots by 2000 Z.

UAL 439	United 439 holding on taxiway L.
15 Ground	United 439, hold position. There's an aircraft de-icer at stand 62 blocking your stand. BA Bus Number 5, where are you?
Bus 5	Stand 52, waiting to depart. Number 5 Bus.
Ground	Roger, BA bus. Hang on. I've got a fire tender outbound at taxiway B, repeat B.
Bus 5	Roger that. Holding.
RYR 372	Ryanair 372 request push back stand 53.
Ground	Push back approved, 372.
UAL 439	United 439 holding on taxiway L. Is there a problem at stand 63?
Ground	Hold position, 439. There's a maintenance truck leaving your stand. Ryanair 355 proceed to intersection MA, hold short of the runway. Expect delay. A sweeper is still clearing runway 05.
UAL 439	United 439 holding on L.
Ground	Stand by, 439.
RYR 355	Ryanair 355 holding short of runway 05.
Ground	355, line up and wait. The sweeper is leaving the runway. Cleared for take-off.
RYR 355	Cleared for take-off, Ryanair 355.

Ground	Tug 3, report when ready to vacate stand 6. Lufthansa 158 approaching.
16 KLM 219	Ground, KLM 219 runway 24 clear. Holding. Listen, can I change stand? I have to be near our maintenance area. I have a flat tyre on the nose gear.
Ground	KLM, 219, do you need a push-back tug?
Tug 3	Hang on a minute. Hello. Hello. I can't hear. I've got a radio problem. Tug 3.
Ground	Lufthansa 158, slow down, taxi slowly to intersection D4. KLM 219, stand by. Tug 3, vacate stand 6. Report.
DLH 158	Taxiing slowly. Stand 6 in sight and still blocked. Request stand change. Lufthansa 158.
KLM 219	KLM 219, still holding. Did you get my message? Confirm stand, please.
Tug 3	Ground, read you now. Stand 6 vacated. Tug 3.
Ground	Roger Tug 3. Lufthansa 158, stand 6 is cleared. Proceed straight ahead. Break break KLM 219, hold position. Give way to 757 on taxiway Z.
KLM 219	Holding postion, KLM 219.
DLH 158	Stand 6 confirmed. Lufthansa 158.
Ground	KLM 219, stand 19 is clear. A maintenance truck is on its way for your flat. Taxi with caution due to works. Keep well to the left.
KLM 219	Stand 19. Hey, I can see lots of works. Request closest available stand. KLM 219.

Ground	This is it, KLM confirm stand 19.
Works 24	Ground, request proceed to construction works near stand 19.
Ground	Hold Works 24, stand 19 already has a fuel tanker waiting and a push-back tug there, and I can see heavy plant nearby. Is this urgent Works 24?
Works 24	Negative, Ground. I can wait until the heavy has refuelled.
KLM 219	KLM 219, I don't want to be difficult, but with a flat tyre, I need the nearest stand available. Is that possible?
Ground	Negative. Turn right onto L, taxi with caution, go beyond the works to stand 19. Confirm, KLM 219.
KLM 219	Confirm stand 19. KLM 219.

UNIT 3, EXERCISE 10

🔊 19

1   Be informed. Centreline lights out of order on runway 27.
2   Caution. Construction work at the edge of the taxiway. It's marked by red flags.
3   Be advised. Ice reported at the holding area. Braking action poor. Caution.
4   Be advised. Standing water at the midpoint on the runway.
5   Caution. Slush on stand E40.
6   Be advised. Edge of apron partly covered with gravel opposite the terminal building.

UNIT 3, EXERCISE 13

🔊 20

Ground	Finnair 2115, taxi with caution. A snowplough is proceeding to the intersection.
FIN 2115	Roger. Finnair 2115.
SIA 107	Singapore 107, de-icing finished more than 10 minutes ago. The de-icer trucks have already left. Request immediate start-up to meet my slot time of 25.
Ground	Negative, Singapore 107. You have a new slot time of 40, repeat 40.
SIA 107	Singapore 107, confirm new slot time of 40, but still expect to start-up because de-icing is already done. Can you put me on request for slot before 40?
Ground	Singapore 107, stand by. I'll call you back in a few seconds. Finnair 2115 slow down, hold position at intersection. Snowplough and sweepers at work. Singapore 107, slot time still 40.
SIA 107	Roger. Singapore 107.
FIN 2115	Finnair 2115 taxiing slowly to intersection, but I can see snowplough is just moving off. Should I still hold position?
Ground	Finnair 2115, carry on straight ahead. Caution. Watch out for gusting winds, wind shear reported.

SIA 107	Ground, Singapore 107 request urgent start-up, or I'll have to get de-icing again.
Ground	Negative, Singapore 107. Expect further delays. Snow banks are building up on compacted snow at the end of the taxiway.
SIA 107	How much longer do I have to wait? Singapore 107.
Ground	I'll call you back in a moment, Singapore 107.

UNIT 3, EXERCISE 15

🔊 21

Ground	Speedbird 937, push back approved.
BAW 937	Speedbird 937 is pushing back.
Ground	Roger Speedbird 937, taxi to runway 24 via taxiway B1 to holding point L3. Report holding point L3. Wind 180 degrees, 5 knots. QNH 1010, time 23.
BAW 937	Speedbird 937 to holding point L3 via taxiway ... Speedbird 937 at holding point L3 ready for immediate departure.
Ground	Speedbird 937, maintain position at L3. Wait for landing Airbus 320 to vacate runway 24.
BAW 937	Holding position at L3, waiting for A320 to vacate. Speedbird 937.
Ground	Speedbird 937, line up and hold. Prepare for departure. 937, er, hold position, I say again hold position at L3. Cancel line up. Acknowledge.
BAW 937	Holding position at L3, Speedbird 937.
Ground	Speedbird 937, I can't issue take off clearance. There seems to be a problem. The Airbus 320 has stopped on the runway. Stand by, Speedbird 937.
BAW 937	Roger, Speedbird 937.

UNIT 3, EXERCISE 18

🔊 22

Ground	Speedbird 937, the problem seems to be over. The Airbus 320 is being towed off runway 24 because of a major engine failure. Expect further delay due to sweepers clearing debris. It should take no more than 5 or 6 minutes.
BAW 937	Roger. Speedbird 937.
Ground	Speedbird 937, prepare for immediate departure.
BAW 937	Ready for immediate departure. Speedbird 937.
Ground	Speedbird 937, runway 24 cleared for take off.
BAW 937	Runway 24 cleared for take off. Speedbird 937.

Exchange 1

23

Tower	456, expedite taxi to runway 06 left.
Co-pilot 456	Which holding point are we heading for?
Pilot 456	It's usually A, but I'm taking AG. We get a shorter runway, but it's still OK. I never like this runway. That rise in the middle blocks the view. You can't see the other end until you're at the midpoint.
Tower	456, line up and take off immediately runway 06 left.
Pilot 456	Taking off. Runway 06 left, 456. There are vehicles on the runway!
Co-pilot 456	We'll make it. V1 ... rotate.
Pilot 456	What the hell ...
Co-pilot 456	Looked like works of some sort.
Pilot 456	Control, we've just had a near miss with some vehicles near the end of the runway.
Tower	Yeah, we saw, 456. You cleared them by about 50 feet. You entered the runway at the wrong point. We do not have the full length available today.

Exchange 2

ATC	BVL, for identification purposes, could you turn left heading 340. BVL identified. Maintain flight level 190. After passing GANET turn left heading 270.
BVL	Flight level 190, turn left heading 270. BVL.

Exchange 3

Departure	N355, climb flight level 80.
N355	Climbing flight level 90. N355.
Departure	N355, I say again flight level 80, 80. Keep at flight level 80 due traffic. You're up at 8600 feet already. Descend immediately.
N355	Did you say flight level 80? Are you sure? N355.
Departure	Affirm, N355. Descend immediately. There's inbound traffic at 6 miles now, flight level 90.

Exchange 4

Departure	GBL, airborne 1905. Climb straight ahead heading 050. Report when you're past 5000 feet.
GBL	Roger GBL. Passing 5000 feet. GBL.
Departure	GBL, continue climb flight level 120. No speed restrictions.
Alert	Traffic, traffic. Descend, descend.
GBL	TCAS descend. GBL.
Alert	Clear of conflict.
GBL	Clear of conflict. Level at 5000. GBL.
Departure	GBL, roger. GBL, maintain 5000 feet. Turn right heading 090. GBL, clear of traffic. Heading 350. Continue climb flight level 120 and call on reaching.

GBL	Can you confirm climb back 120? GBL.
Departure	GBL, affirm. Flight level 120. Heading 350. Do you want to file a report?
GBL	Er – affirm ...

Exchange 5

Departure	N3E, what's your level?
N3E	Just out of 5500 for flight level 150. Heading 050. N3E.
Departure	N3E, are you able to level off at 6000 feet?
N3E	Affirm. Maintaining 6000 feet. Can I stay on same heading? N3E.
Departure	N3E, just stay on the same heading for the time being. You have opposite traffic 7000 feet. Expect further climb shortly.

Exchange 6

ATC	D6V, this is en route holding. Make one right hand orbit in your present position and leave on heading 130. Report abeam HOLLY.
D6V	Sorry – we're not very keen on orbiting. Do you mind if we have a level change instead? D6V.
ATC	D6V, stand by for level change. D6V, level change approved. Cleared to 160. Same heading. Expect further clearance at 16. Landing delays at Milan 15 minutes.

Exchange 7

Tower	C23, cleared for take off, wind 085 degrees, 15 knots.
Pilot C23	Cleared for take off, C23.
Co-pilot C23	OK, we've got a red on hydraulics – and on flight controls. Rudder hydraulics on the overhead ... Red's everywhere now. Do you want ...
Tower	C23, abort your take off. Abort your take off. You've got smoke coming from one of your engines. Abort your take off.
Co-pilot C23	Aborting take off. Where's the smoke coming from?
Tower	It appears to be from the central engine by the looks of it – number 2.
Pilot C23	Closing down number 2.

Exchange 1

25
A Did you say you checked the QNH setting?
B Yeah, it's fine.

Exchange 2

A Are you sure you want us to use taxiway X?
B Sorry, no. Taxiway P.

Exchange 3

A Sorry, can we use runway 23 instead of runway 28?
B Yep, that's fine.

Exchange 4

A   Did you say you wanted medical assistance?

B   Yes, please.

Exchange 5

A   Can I change to flight level 350 rather than 310?

B   As you wish. Flight level 350.

Exchange 6

A   Can you confirm you've reached flight level 150?

B   Sure – just approaching 150 now.

UNIT 4, EXERCISE 5

26

Tower	L556, are you ready for departure?
Pilot L556	Ready. L556.
Tower	L556, cleared for take off. Wind 270 degrees, 5 knots.
Pilot L556	Cleared for take off. L556.
Tower	L556, be advised, helicopter at the end of runway 27 left.
Pilot L556	Rolling. We have no visual contact. No helicopter in sight. L556.
Tower	L556, yes sir. Helicopter at the end of the runway. He's just come from the north. Continue departure.
Pilot L556	We have no visual with helicopter. Are you sure? L556.
Tower	Ah – L556, the helicopter is above the runway, sir.
Pilot L556	What? He's not even on the ground?
Co-pilot L556	Ah! I've got him. No conflict. Over there, look! He's hovering about 100 feet up at 3 o'clock. Across the airfield near the chimney. Just in front of that large building.
Pilot L556	Where?
Co-pilot L556	Well over to the right. Beyond the car park, behind the trees, next to the chimney. In fact if he gets any closer he'll bump into it! It's fine. No problem. He's well below our path.

UNIT 4, EXERCISE 9

27

Communication 1

YB, look out for slow-moving traffic 6 miles ahead of you. You'll pass over him.

Communication 2

YB, avoiding action. Turn left immediately, heading 270 degrees, opposite traffic at 12 o'clock.

Communication 3

YB, traffic on your left. 6 miles overtaking. Same level.

Communication 4

YB, be informed. Fast-moving traffic at 2 o'clock, 6 miles crossing right to left. 1000 feet below.

Communication 5

YB, conflicting traffic at 9 o'clock.

Communication 6

YB, traffic 3 o'clock, 8 miles parallel. DC10 1000 feet below, climbing.

Communication 7

YB, maintain flight level 80 due converging traffic 10 o'clock, 15 miles, 1000 feet below. Maintain 80 until further advised.

Communication 8

YB, you're well clear of traffic. He's diverging away from you. In your 2 o'clock position.

UNIT 4, EXERCISE 12

29

ATC	B550, we have a report of some vapour streaming aft of you.
B550	Tumbiki Control, thanks. Sounds like we're losing some fuel. We're declaring an emergency. Returning to Tumbiki. B550.
ATC	B550, roger. Do you want to dump any fuel?
B550	Affirmative. I'll have to get rid of some. I can't risk any overheating of the brake units. And I certainly don't want any fuel spilling onto hot brakes. B550.
ATC	B550, do you require any airport services?
B550	Affirmative. I need some protection, please. Fire and rescue services required. B550.

UNIT 5, EXERCISE 1

30

1   Be informed. Weather balloon drifting across your path from right to left. Level unknown, but it's approximately 4 miles north-east of your current position.

2   Caution. Obstacle warning light on top of Marchwood Power Station inoperable.

3   Be advised. Fuel dumping in progress 20 miles east of Aberdeen. Eastbound. Flight level 100. Avoid flight within 5 miles at this level. If within 5 miles remain at least 1000 above or 2000 feet below this aircraft.

4   Be informed. In-flight refuelling in progress 5 miles south of Land's End. Likely to continue until 1500 UTC.

5   Fireworks display within 1 mile radius of Exeter, Devon. Planned start time is 2000 and is expected to last 30 minutes. On site contact 791615.

Communication 1
31 Be advised. Hang gliding competition at Merthyr. Original start time was 0900 Z. This is now delayed and restrictions for other traffic will become effective at 1115 Z and remain in force until 2059 Z.

Communication 2
Free-fall drop zone established at Land's End 1.5 miles radius of 5006.17N, 0054.023W up to flight level 150. Drop time 1000 UTC. Be advised that there are 2 jump ships cruising at 90 knots, crossing the airway from right to left. Because of the large numbers involved, traffic restrictions have been extended until 1100 UTC.

Communication 3
Be advised. Fighter training over Brecon Beacons was due to start at 1330. This has been brought forward and restrictions will now take effect from 1200 and will last until 2200.

Communication 4
Be advised. The Bath hot air balloon event scheduled for 1000 UTC until 1300 UTC is starting late. Start time is now 1100 UTC and traffic restrictions will be suspended until 1030 UTC. They will now remain in force until 1400 UTC. Expect mass launches of hot air balloons. Up to 35 balloons may participate during each 30 minute launch period and may be found up to 20 miles downwind of launch sites. Pilots are requested to exercise caution in the vicinity. Controlled airspace will be avoided unless approved by ATC.

Communication 5
Laser testing finished early at 0930 UTC, so traffic restrictions in the Hatfield area cancelled.

Exchange 1
33 *B333*	We didn't expect it so bumpy up here! Would you check if there's any traffic ahead of us? We may need better separation. B333.
ATC	B333, affirm. You have traffic ahead. It's a 747. Must be wake turbulence. Would you like a higher level?
B333	Affirm. We'd certainly like a more comfortable ride. B333.
ATC	B333, roger. Climb flight level 270 – it should be free of turbulence. Expect further climb at 45. If you have any further problems, please advise.

Exchange 2
Buck 36	Er, we've got a problem. This is the slowest climb out ever! We've lost engine number 1.
Alert	Bank angle, bank angle.
Departure	Buck 36, something large has fallen off your plane.

Buck 36	This is more serious than I thought. Declare an emergency.
Departure	Buck 36, are you returning to Lohoa?
Buck 36	Roger. Returning. Buck 36.

Exchange 3
AF-39	Control, request diversion to the nearest airport. AF-39.
ATC	AF-39, understand you are requesting diversion.
AF-39	Affirm.
ATC	AF-39, turn left heading 270. Can you give me a reason for the diversion?
AF-39	Sure. We have a smell of exhaust fumes in the cockpit.
ATC	Is there any smoke?
AF-39	Negative. No smoke, but the smell is getting stronger. AF-39.
ATC	Roger. Continue heading and contact 118.6.

Exchange 1
34 *B333*	OK – we're fine at this level. Next time please give us at least 6 miles behind a heavy. B333.

Exchange 2
Buck 36	We're turning back to Lohoa. I think it was the engine ... the engine fell off.
Departure	Buck 36, say your intentions.
Buck 36	We are going to maintain this heading. We're having problems with speed and with flight controls. Buck 36.
Departure	Buck 36, roger. Choose your runway. We'll clear everything. Are you able to maintain terrain clearance?
Buck 36	Affirmative. We are maintaining 1500 feet. We need to get rid of fuel. Buck 36.
Departure	Buck 36, roger.
Buck 36	All right. I want runway 6 left.
Departure	Buck 36, runway 6 left, cleared to land.
Buck 36	All right. All right. We're landing 6 left. Buck 36.
Departure	Buck 36, all the gear appears good.
Buck 36	Thank you. Buck 36. Heh-heh ... we did it!
Departure	Affirm 36. You did a good job!

Exchange 3
AF39	Pan-pan, pan-pan, pan-pan, Fairview Tower. Fumes in cockpit. Request priority landing. AF-39 pan-pan.
Tower	AF-39 pan-pan, Fairview Tower. You are number one. Cleared to land. Straight in. Runway 17, wind 170 degrees, eight knots. QNH 1008. Fire service requested.
AF-39	Runway 17, QNH 1008, AF-39 pan-pan.
Tower	Take first right when vacated. Contact Fire Service directly on 118.5.
AF-39	First right, 118.5. AF-39 pan-pan.

FS1	AF-39, Fire Service 1. Suggest you evacuate your passengers as soon as possible, sir. Fire Service 1.
AF-39	Do I need an emergency evacuation, Fire Service 1? We've still got a strong smell of fumes – we may have an oil leak somewhere.
FS1	Negative, AF-39. That won't be necessary. The passengers can disembark normally. The bus is just pulling up now to take them to the terminal. We'll come on board as soon as you're all clear. Fire Service 1.

UNIT 5, EXERCISE 14

Exchange 1

35

Pilot	We have a passenger with severe chest pain and is clearly not at all well. We've got him on oxygen.
Doctor	OK, is the pain a really crushing pain? Maybe moving into his jaw or left arm?
Pilot	Yes.
Doctor	Shortness of breath?
Pilot	Yes.
Doctor	Have you worked out if …

Exchange 2

Pilot	We have a problem with a diabetic patient. He's quite aggressive, but his wife assures us it's because he's diabetic. Apparently he took his insulin before coming on board as he was expecting to eat shortly afterwards. We were delayed though and sat on the tarmac for an hour and a half so he hasn't eaten. His wife is very worried …

Exchange 3

Pilot	We have a passenger who's had a seizure and the cabin crew are very concerned. She's epileptic apparently. It started off with some twitching of her face and hands, but it's gradually got worse and worse. Her arms and legs have been jerking all over the place. She seems to have stopped that now, but she's not awake.
Doctor	OK – it's not uncommon for an epileptic to lose consciousness. Maybe even for a few minutes. Just make sure she's comfortable and cannot fall and hurt herself …

Exchange 4

Pilot	We have a distressed passenger. He's asthmatic and has packed his inhaler in the hold. We don't appear to have a doctor on board. This guy's having lots of trouble breathing.
Doctor	Don't worry that you haven't got a doctor. It's quite manageable. You should find an inhaler in your own medical kit. He'll know how to use it if he uses one regularly …

Exchange 5

Pilot	We have a passenger – a young boy – with really nasty stomach pains. The crew are very worried it may be appendicitis. If it is, will we have to divert?
Doctor	It's certainly possible, but tell me why they think it's appendicitis.
Pilot	Well – it's really painful – the poor kid's in agony. The face is really red.
Doctor	Did it come on suddenly?
Pilot	It seems to have done.
Doctor	And is it made worse by movement?
Pilot	Definitely. And his stomach's like a board …

Exchange 6

Doctor	Do you require medical assistance?
Pilot	Yes, we do, thank you. We've got a passenger who's fallen and cut his head badly. He's bleeding a lot and there's blood everywhere – he's got a massive bruise all down the side of his face, too.
Doctor	Has he lost consciousness at all – or is he just …

UNIT 6, EXERCISE 1

Part 1

36

Big-B 276	Big-B 276. Wessex Approach. Joining the hold. Maintaining 8000 feet.
Approach	276, maintain 8000 feet. We are experiencing some delays here.
Big-B 276	What's the problem? 276.
Approach	276, I'm sorry, sir – we had delays earlier today. We had some jet blast damage just behind the threshold. It took a long time to clear it all. That's why everyone's backed up.
Big-B 276	So how long can I expect to wait? I need to get down before 2300, don't I?
Approach	Indeed you do, sir. Noise abatement regulations are very strict here. At the moment it's a bit difficult to say – delays will be about half an hour, at least.

Part 2

Big-B 276	Wessex Approach. Big-B 276. Can you give me an update?
Approach	I think you may be waiting quite a while. I'll get back to you shortly. You can now descend in the hold to 6000 feet. Report passing 7000. And if you could reduce to – er – 180 – that'd be good. Just for a bit of spacing from the one ahead of you.
Big-B 276	Roger. Out of 8000 feet for 6000 feet. 276.

Part 3

Approach	Big-B 276, Wessex Approach. I'm sorry sir, but I'm going to have to divert you to Exeter. There isn't time to get you on the

ground before the night noise curfew takes effect. Climb immediately to 9000 feet heading …

UNIT 6, EXERCISE 5

Good evening, ladies and gentlemen. This is the captain again. I apologize for the delay this evening. I'm afraid there are severe delays at Wessex due to air traffic. Wessex has got a noise abatement curfew, so we can't land after 11 p.m. We've been diverted to Exeter. Please accept our sincere apologies for the inconvenience. We know this will mess up a lot of your plans. The cabin crew will continue to look after you until we reach Exeter. Ground staff in Exeter will be available to make sure you reach your final destination as soon as possible.

UNIT 6, EXERCISE 8

Exchange 1

Tower	Alitalia 29, if you could come back to final approach speed – there are a couple of aircraft want to get off ahead of you.
AZA 29	We're just below 300 metres.
Tower	I'm just waiting for one to get airborne. OK, keep a high speed as much as you can all the way down.

Exchange 2

AFL 339	Aeroflot 339. Heading 090 will not take us to the localizer. We should need to turn to the right, turning right heading 110 to establish.
Tower	OK, the radar shows you just about on the centreline now, but you can adjust your heading as required.

Exchange 3

Tower	Speedbird 34, if you're able – reduce to about – er – 190. Continue heading 250.

Exchange 4

DLH 1390	Lufthansa 1390, we are visual. Requesting visual approach. We've got the Aeroflot traffic above us slightly to the left.
Tower	OK, he's going around. You're number 2 in the sequence and you're cleared for a visual right hand runway 10.

Exchange 5

Tower	Austrian 26, OK, you can't land from this approach now. I've put someone ahead of you. Just continue on track 009, please. I'll give you further vectors back to the ILS.

Exchange 6

Tower	Speedbird 440, you're identified. What's your passing altitude?

UNIT 6, EXERCISE 9

KLM 405	Petersburg Approach. KLM 405.
Approach	KLM 405, Petersburg Approach. Maintain altitude 2400 metres.
KLM 405	KLM 405. Maintaining altitude 2400 metres.
Approach	Report KE, KLM 405.
KLM 405	KE time 26, altitude 2400 metres. Estimating OLSON 28. Request descent.
Approach	KLM 405, descend altitude 1500 metres.
KLM 405	Descending 1500 metres. KLM 405.
Approach	Maintain altitude 1500 metres, QNH 1008. Report speed 405.
KLM 405	220 knots reducing to 190 knots, 1008. KLM 405.
Approach	Roger, KLM 405.

UNIT 6, EXERCISES 10–11

Information Romeo: 2000 Z 800, scattered, visibility 14 kilometres, temperature 44, wind 310, 8 knots, altimeter 30.00, expect ILS or visual to runway 24 and 33, advise on first contact you have information Romeo.

UNIT 6, EXERCISE 13

Approach	KLM 405, continue heading 270, descend 900 metres, reduce speed 180 knots, and report outer marker for runway 28 left.
KLM 405	Heading 270, descend 900 metres, reduce speed 180 knots, will report outer marker for runway 28 left. KLM 405.
Approach	KLM 405, be advised of wet conditions on runway 28 left. A mix of slush and rain. Lots of standing water.
KLM 405	Approach, can I change runway? KLM 405.
Approach	Negative. Reports of wet conditions are not critical, but adjust your speed, 405.
KLM 405	I'm pretty heavy. Listen, I'm overshooting. 405.
Approach	Confirm 405, are you going around?
KLM 405	Affirm. 405 is going around, I say again going around.
Approach	Understood 405 going around. Climb straight ahead …

UNIT 6, EXERCISE 14

KLM 405	Approach, KLM 405, established on ILS 28 right. What's the situation with the runway?
Approach	KLM 405, surface conditions no better, no worse. Runway wet, slush in patches, there's slight aquaplaning reported, braking action good. Continue approach on ILS, you are number 2, number 1 is touching down. Be sure to check your speed on final.
KLM 405	Thanks. Continuing approach, KLM 405.

UNIT 6, EXERCISE 16

AA 745	Bradley Approach, American 745 at 8000 feet with Romeo.
Approach	Roger, American 745. Heading 330. Descend to 5000 feet, vectors to runway 33, traffic pattern for the visual approach.
AA 745	Approach, American 745. We have you in sight.
Approach	Cleared for visual approach runway 33. Uh, hang on, American 745. We got quite a bit of traffic here today. Do you mind going for runway 24?
AA 745	Runway 24? No problem.
Approach	OK, set up downwind for 24, steer 060, American 745.
AA 745	Affirmative, we'll go runway 24. I also need a favour. The crew have just reported a sick passenger. Would you organize an ambulance on arrival?
Approach	Affirm, American 745. There's an A320 ahead of you on 2 mile short final. Well ahead of you. You are number 2. Cleared for visual approach runway 24. Contact Tower on 120.20.
AA 745	Good evening Bradley Tower, American 745 downwind for 24.
Tower	American 745, cleared to land.
AA 745	Cleared to land. American 745.

UNIT 6, EXERCISE 18

Tower	F22, Newbury Tower. Turn right heading 060. Reduce speed to 180 knots.
WHF-22	Turning right heading 060. Speed now 200 knots. Turning base leg. F22.
Tower	F22, cleared altitude 2500 feet. Say again 2500 feet. You're already lower than that. You must stay above 2500 feet.
WHF-22	2500. F22. 2500.
Tower	F22, yes – you're still too low – you have to be above 2500 feet. If you could climb back up to 2500 please and turn right now onto 120 degrees.
WHF-22	Turning 120. F22.
Tower	F22, you are still descending! You must climb now. Climb 2500 feet.
WHF-22	2500 feet. F22.
Tower	F22, climb immediately. There is a mast 4 miles due east of your current position. Height is 1300 feet. When you get to it, it'll be higher than you. F22, QNH 982. Can you confirm you are indicating 1500?
WHF-22	Just got it now and climbing. Reading 2000 feet. F22.
Tower	F22, you can level off at 2000 feet please to intercept the glidepath at 7 miles. You are now clear of the TV mast.

UNIT 7, EXERCISE 5

Pilot 105	There's no ECAM message so why don't you check the handbook now, so we can work out how to get this thing down safely.
ATC	Would you like me to put you through to your company?
Co-pilot 105	Possibly. Perhaps you could give me a few minutes to check the handbook and then call back?
ATC	Roger. I'll call you back in 2 minutes, shall I?
Co-pilot 105	Thanks.
Pilot 105	We've no idea whether the whole of the nose gear is damaged. I think we ought to assume it may all collapse when we land.
Co-pilot 105	Sure – landing with abnormal gear – here it is. First problem is that if the gear collapses then both engine nacelles will contact the runway.
Pilot 105	Couldn't we shut down just as we land?
Co-pilot 105	Yeah – ... but – you'd better shut down for sure, but I don't think you should leave it too late though. The procedure is to shut down before or during the landing roll. I know you want all the services as long as possible but if I were you, I'd shut down sooner rather than later.

UNIT 7, EXERCISE 7

ATC	SAS 105, your company engineers have requested a low pass to inspect the gear. You could do that as soon as you're ready. The engineers will give you a visual inspection of the landing gear.
Pilot 105	Roger. Sounds good. Why don't we come down to about 500 feet?
ATC	OK, try it. Fly level past the runway threshold.
Pilot 105	Roger. OK – we're at 500 feet.
ATC	Yeah, we know. It's not low enough. The gear's down but we need a much closer look. What about going down to 300 feet?
Pilot 105	Shall I go down to 200?
ATC	OK, yes. I think you should because it's really difficult to see much at the moment. OK, OK, that's great. Yeah – left nose wheel is definitely missing but the right nose wheel is in place. So, heading 320 climb to 3000 feet. You'll get onward clearance shortly to rejoin the holding stack.
Pilot 105	Roger.

49

	Approach	SAS 105, what's the fuel situation?
	Co-pilot 105	We're at maximum weight but I don't want to wait any longer. It'll be dark soon. SAS 105.
	Approach	OK, SAS 105. I know you didn't specifically request foam, but expect foam carpet in approximately 15 minutes. How many passengers aboard?
	Co-pilot 105	237 plus 8 crew. All services needed. SAS 105.
	Approach	Roger, 105. SAS 105, cleared for straight-in approach. Runway 06 left. Wind 025, 10 knots. QNH 1008. Fire services advised.
	Co-pilot 105	105 is established.
	Approach	105, continue to reduce speed. The foam carpet begins 500 metres after the threshold and continues for further 700 metres. 15 metres wide.
	Co-pilot 105	Roger. 105.

50

Exchange 1

Pilot	What are runway conditions like?
Approach	Braking action is poor and there's heavy slush reported at the far end of the runway.

Exchange 2

Approach	Varig 107, please note some of the centreline lights are missing in the approach lighting.
Pilot	107 roger, you can turn off the sequence flashers. The runway is beautifully clear. In fact you can turn the other lights down. They're a bit bright.
Approach	OK, wilco.

Exchange 3

Approach	EZ250, heavy rain and strong crosswinds reported. Caution. Wind shear on short final.

Exchange 4

ATC	Reduce speed to 140 to avoid running into vortex wake of the A320 ahead of you.

Exchange 5

GAB	Pan-pan, pan-pan, pan-pan, Bellevue Approach, GAB 737, request emergency medical support on landing for passenger with suspected heart attack. Number 4 to land on straight-in approach.
ATC	Roger, GAB pan-pan, after landing can you make it to stand 17 – the nearest available?
GAB	What's the distance?
ATC	It'll take about 12 minutes after vacating the runway, GAB pan-pan.
GAB	Don't think so …

52

Ground	American 99 Heavy, Ground. Left turn on 22 right, left turn at F, right turn B.
AAL 99	We were given our gate earlier, if it's still open, but we need to get past the 757 in front of us.
Ground	99 Heavy, you can go behind the 727 and continue. Gate 47 is all clear.
AAL 99	It's a 757, Ground.
Ground	Oh, OK. Sorry, my strip says 727.
AAL 99	No problem. Taxiing to gate 47, American 99.
Ground	Delta 31, continue A, hold short of M.
DAL 31	A short of M, Delta 31.
Ground	921 Heavy, you're short of MA?
921	Yes sir, just short of MA. We're cleared into the gate.
Ground	Taxi to ramp, good day. Delta 31, give way to the A320 entering taxiway A5. Then continue to MA. Your stand is 54.
DAL 31	Ground, the A320 is already past. Ready to roll, proceeding to MA. Gate 54, Delta 31.
Maint. 21	Ground, Maintenance 21, stand 27. Request proceed to work in progress taxiway L.
Ground	Stand by, Maintenance 21. Jetblue are you with me again? OK, Maintenance 21 proceed to taxiway L via Z and A.
Maint. 21	Proceeding to taxiway L via Z and A, Maintenance 21.
Ground	Jetblue, are you back with me again? Jetblue, are you the one who reported the number of the truck crossing at the intersection? Just standby one second, OK.
CCA 982	China 982, holding ready to taxi.
Ground	I'm sorry, hold China 982. Sorry, Freedom Air, say again.
CCA 982	Air China 982 holding.
Ground	Yes, Air China, I heard you. Who's the Freedom Air calling?
FOM 6182	Freedom 6182 being blocked by Air China, M short of AN.
Ground	6182, I have your request, stand by. Air China what did you want?
CCA 982	Air China 982 holding.
Ground	OK Jetblue, what happened with the truck?
JBU	We came out of W, turned right, and were crossed by a truck. I noted the number. It was 1097.
Ground	You think it was a flat-bed – 1097, mostly white?
JBU	Absolutely, it was … er … it was a tractor pulling a flatbed.
CCA 982	China 982 ready to taxi.
Ground	Ground, China 982, I heard you. Stand by.
CCA 982	Holding. China 982.

JBU	It was crossing right at the WA intersection. I'd appreciate you reporting.
Ground	Air China left turn on 22 right, left turn at F, right turn B to stand 56.
CCA 982	Turn right on 22 right, left turn at …
Ground	Negative Air China 982, turn left, repeat left on 22 right, then left at F, right turn B. Acknowledge.
CCA 982	China 982 turn left on 22 right, then left at F, turn right B.
Ground	Freedom 6182, wait for Air China heavy to vacate 22 right. Then continue, turn right at F. Your gate is 52. Caution, construction work at end of gate.
FOM 6182	Freedom 6182 taxiing, right turn at F, proceeding to gate 52, caution construction work at 52.

OXFORD
UNIVERSITY PRESS

Great Clarendon Street, Oxford OX2 6DP

Oxford University Press is a department of the University of Oxford.
It furthers the University's objective of excellence in research, scholarship,
and education by publishing worldwide in

Oxford New York

Auckland Cape Town Dar es Salaam Hong Kong Karachi
Kuala Lumpur Madrid Melbourne Mexico City Nairobi
New Delhi Shanghai Taipei Toronto

With offices in

Argentina Austria Brazil Chile Czech Republic France Greece
Guatemala Hungary Italy Japan Poland Portugal Singapore
South Korea Switzerland Thailand Turkey Ukraine Vietnam

OXFORD and OXFORD ENGLISH are registered trade marks of
Oxford University Press in the UK and in certain other countries

ISBN: 978 0 19 457943 8

Printed in China

This book is printed on paper from certified and well-managed sources.

ACKNOWLEDGEMENTS

*The publisher would like to thank the following for their kind permission to
reproduce photographs and other copyright material*: Alamy pp 5 (pilot
daytime/G P Bowater), (copilot/David R. Frazier Photolibrary,Inc.),
(cabin crew/Picture Contact), (passengers/mediacolors), 8 (David Noton
Photography), 9 (AGStockUSA,Inc.), 11 (runway/Richard Cooke), (aeroplane/
Steven May), 13 (helicopter/Andrew Stevens), 19 (stormclouds/A.T.Willett),
(earthquake crack/mediacolors), (snowdrift/Pixonnet.com), (rain/
ImageState), (hail/Vadym Kharkivskiy), 20 (Picture Contact), 29 (aeroplane
takeoff/Anthony Kay), 37 (biplanes/David Osborn), (weather balloon/
David R. Frazier Photolibrary, Inc.), (fuel dumping/Dave Pattison), (in-flight
refuelling/Transtock Inc.), 39 (plane on runway/Elmtree Images), (plane
in flight/Anthony Nettle), (vintage plane/Mark Baigent), 44 (Coaster), 67
(A380/Anthony Nettle); Photo (c) BAA Limited pp 5 (air traffic controller),
13 (Airbus A300), (gulfstream jet), 29 (fog), (repairs), 53; Copyright (c)
Boeing p 67 (boeing); Thomas Bracx p 60 (Transat); Courtesy Cessna
Aircraft Company p 13 (Cessna Skycatcher); Corbis cover (aeroplane
sunset/moodboard), (runway sunset/Bob Krist), pp 12 (moodboard), 19
(windswept trees/Jim Reed), 57 (George Steinmetz); Getty Images cover
(cockpit/Michael Dunning); Norbert Gratzer p 55; Stephen Innes/
Aerocorp International p 13 (amphibious plane); (c) iStockphoto.com
pp 7 (kkgas), 19 (volcano plume/subemontes), (sandstorm/pancaketom),
37 (explosion/icholakov), (hanglider/BirdofPrey), (skydiver/Fly_Fast),
45 (halbergman), 67 (woman with scarf/VikramRaghuvanshi), (woman
with grey hair/YinYang); (c) Jeppesen Sanderson, Inc. 2008 p 49;
Reproduced with permission of Jeppesen Sanderson, Inc. NOT FOR
NAVIGATIONAL USE; Heather Marsden p 43; Willem Johannes Meyer
p 35; morgueFile pp 13 (Airbus A380/o0o0xmods0o0o), 19 (birds/
rollingroscoe), (slush/Kevin Connors); Oxford Unversity Press pp 37 (hot
air balloons/Comstock), 67 (young man curly hair/Digital Vision), (older
man/Photodisc), (young blond man/Gareth Boden), (brown haired boy/
Steve Skjold); PunchStock p 5 (cockpit/image100).

Illustrations by: Peter Richards pp 40, 42, 71, 73; Peters & Zabransky UK
Ltd pp 14, 15, 17, 21, 22, 23, 25, 27, 29, 31, 32, 34, 47, 59, 61, 62, 63, 64,
70, 72

*The authors and publishers would like to thank the following teachers and
aviation professionals who assisted in the development of this book*: Dilso C.
de Almeida, Aviation English Teacher, DCA Learning; Cécile Blazejczak-
Boulegue, B-737 First Officer, Europe Airpost; Alexandra Burow, English
Language Lecturer, Emirates Aviation College; Yuliya Cheprassova, Pseudo-
pilot for ATC simulators training; Cybele Gallo, Language Rater, Brazilian
CAA, and aviation English teacher; Teresa Greco, Istituto Tecnico Orion;
Stephen Innes, Chief Pilot, Aerocorp International, and International
Operations and Planning, Bombardier Aerospace; Ron Jenkins, Consultant
to the Joint Aviation Authorities, and Director, Global Aviation Language
Limited; Robert Mathews, Coordinator, Qatar Aeronautical College; Gábor
Sipos, language expert, Budapest; Nancy Young, English Trainer, French
Civil Aviation

*The authors would like to thank Lewis Lansford for all his help in the preparation
of this course.*